STAY FOCUSED, REMAIN HUMBLE & KEEP WORKING

BRYAN MAJORS

TRAINING FOR
TRIUMPH

HOW TO PREPARE MENTALLY, PHYSICALLY, EMOTIONALLY & SPIRITUALLY FOR YOUR LIFE LONG GOALS

Training for Triumph
Published by MAJOR PREP, LLC

ISBN 9781730977886
First Printing November 2018, 2nd Edition Printed December 2018
Printed in the United States of America
10 9 8 7 6 5 4 3 2 1
Proofread By: Merry Grace Majors & Cece Pharris
Edited By: Kelia Olughu
Major Prep LLC
www.bryanmajors.com
Instagram: @majorpreplifestyle @majorprep_apparel
Twitter: majorprep717
Facebook: Major Preparation

Table of Contents

Praise for Training for Triumph

"... highly 'readable' and motivating for young readers because of your willingness to be vulnerable with the "good and bad" experiences in your life and with the personal stories that back up your principles for "life growth. You captured the importance of a strong father's guidance in all aspects of life, as well as the "listening" and respect of a mother's love! From setting your spiritual and personal goals through defining back up plans for success, you never lost sight of your firm belief in a loving, caring Heavenly Father who wants the very best for you! Your work (both your life and book) are evidence of what persistence and determination through the support and modeling of family and mentors can do to make you a "MAJOR" difference in the lives of other young men and women! It is a book that teachers, coaches, parents, and mentors can use and give to young teens, students and athletes with whom they live and work as a guide to living a successful life, with each chapter laying out a blueprint that is workable as you so amply illustrate with your own life stories! I love it!

You will always be one of my favorite students at SU! I remember the first day we connected in that early Intro to Ed course when we discovered we both graduated from Harrisburg (John Harris)!

Thank you for giving me this opportunity to read your first book! Blessings! MJ"

--MJ Fair, Associate Pastor and Retired College Professor

FOREWORD

Bryan "B.Maj" Majors is one of the rarest men I've gotten the privilege to know. I consider him a brother and a valued friend. Bryan and I first met thirteen years ago in a Harrisburg, Pennsylvania restaurant. We were both seniors in high school and being heavily recruited to play college basketball. I don't remember a great deal about our meeting that night other than we were both fairly quiet as the coaches sold us on Susquehanna University. They told us that we were going to be running mates for the next four years, and what they envisioned we could achieve together. Neither of us knew if we were going to attend Susquehanna University and become teammates. Fast forward to the middle of that summer after high school graduation, and we'd both committed to play at Susquehanna University.

It was mid-June, and I found myself sitting on a bench outside of the Harrisburg Greyhound station, sweaty and cooking under a relentless sun. An assistant coach was supposed to come and pick me up but claimed instead that he'd sent someone to pick me up. After sitting outside for a few hours, I lost my patience and hoped that a ride was coming to take me back to campus. I sat there with nothing to do, as I blew up the coach's phone. I was hot in every sense of the word. I remember letting this be known to our negligent assistant coach. He paused me, mid-angry-rant, and said he had an idea and that he'd call me back.

Before I heard back from him and after I'd sweated out a t-shirt or two, I looked up and saw Bryan driving towards me. He was smiling and had Lil Wayne's "The Dedication" playing in the background. I hopped in, and he took me over to Perkins for lunch. We still didn't know each other very well. After lunch, Bryan told me he'd give me a tour of his city, and this is when I started to understand the environment that bred him and his brothers. I was first stricken by the fact that regardless of what neighborhood we rode through, everybody had love for him. It didn't matter if we were in a visibly safe area or we were in a part of the city where they'd shot out the streetlights. We'd pass by a corner, or a stoop, or a porch jam-packed with people, and Bryan would pull over, and they'd practically stampede toward the car like he was the ice cream man. He would honk the horn, and the place would erupt into a chorus of folks yelling, "B.Maj!"

I remember asking him how he had the pass in every neighborhood, and he answered, "I try and keep my plate clean with everybody." It was a sentiment I committed to my inner constitution immediately.

Next, he took me to his house, a place where it was easy to feel the love and warmth. I hadn't been in the house very long before Bryan's father, Mr. Majors, greeted me. As soon as he introduced himself, he said he had to ask me a few questions, questions that anyone who wanted to eat in his house needed to answer. He asked me to recite The Lord's Prayer, to name all of the planets in the solar system, to tell him all of the parts of speech and how many letters were in the alphabet. They were very basic questions. I didn't get everything right on my first try, but I did eventually. I quickly understood that Bryan was raised to have morals and a code in the same manner in which I had.

I remember his father driving us to campus the next day and speaking into our lives. He told us how strong of a network we'd be able to build if we didn't quit school. He said we wouldn't be jailbirds. He described for us a vision of a life we both wanted to see, and over the past 12 years, we've supported each other as we climbed the ranks, respectively.

So, after freshman year, it became clear that my passion for basketball was fading while B.Maj was just beginning to walk in the direction of his passion for basketball and training. Though we both played four years on the varsity basketball team at Susquehanna University, I'll be remembered more as a writer, while B.Maj is Susquehanna's all-time leader in steals. Bryan has a big personality, but in the field, he leads by example. The summer going into our junior year of college, I was home in Boston when I got the text that Mr. Majors had passed away. The following season, B.Maj lead our team to the conference finals. This was another moment when I learned about the resilience and toughness Bryan possessed.

At first, people didn't really take my wanting to be a writer seriously, as many people initially scoffed at anyone's dream or aspiration. Bryan knew that I took writing seriously, and he respected it. This leads me to one of the lowest moments of our senior season for myself personally. It was early in the season, and I had a meeting with our head coach, and he basically told me that I hadn't really gotten better as a basketball player over the last four years. Of course, this wasn't true, and it was more of an emotional statement on our coach's part, but I was again fired up. I remember telling Bryan that day at practice that I was going to quit the team. He understood where I was coming from logically speaking. I was deep in the throes of writing my first novel and taking 52 credits to graduate. He heard me out as we were the only two seniors on the team.

Later that night, I remember him texting me something to the effect of: "I know you have way bigger things to do with writing, but we started something. Let's finish it."

We did.

Bryan and I made a success pact together, and we've supported each other over the years as we've run the race. We graduated from college together in four years, and two years later, we both graduated from graduate school. So, when Bryan told me that he was writing a book, I was honored to be writing the foreword. Bryan is a tireless worker, propelled by his passion. I've learned a lot from playing alongside him and watched his continued growth over the years. I couldn't be any more proud to be a part of a project pact with such wisdom.

It has been my pleasure and privilege to have access to the mind and principles of Bryan "B.Maj" Majors. This book gives you that same access. It will educate you. It will inspire you. It will unlock the tools within you to "Train for Triumph." Congratulations in advance on your upcoming success. With this book as a guide, there's no way you won't win!

--Marcus Burke, Author & College Professor

LET THE JOURNEY BEGIN!!!

History/Bio

Excuse me. You asked my name? My name is Bryan Majors. I am a proud product of Gary Westburn Majors and Merry-Grace Majors. I was born and raised in the heart of Harrisburg, PA, where the saying is, "if you can make it here, you can make it anywhere because there's no love here." I repeatedly heard this phrase, so I often took it into consideration. The weight of that quote was often leveled by another quote I'd hear. "It doesn't matter who you are or where you're from. You can become whoever you set your mind to become." Out of both phrases, I chose to align with the latter. The person who told me that was the man I had always looked up to, a man who was my hero, and the man who was the closest thing to God in my eyes. This man was my father.

I am a proud, radiant reflection of my parents, brothers, uncles, the St. Paul Warriors, Hard 2 Guard, Harrisburg Cougars, and the City of Harrisburg. So many people saw the potential in me early on in my life. I always felt extremely blessed to have been surrounded by those who always had my best interest at heart. So many 'old heads' showed me the game on how to maneuver in life that I would have been a fool not to listen to them and be open to receiving my blessings. I always say, "You can do it the hard way or the easy way, but either way, life is going to happen." That was in regard to life in general. Although it seems easier, the hard way consists of being hard-headed, lacking respect, not learning from mistakes, not believing in God, failing to get good grades early, falling into peer pressure, doing or selling drugs, and not doing what is asked of you. The harder way, which inevitably yields the right results, entails acting and behaving the total opposite - listening and doing things the first time you are told, being respectful to any and all adults, learning from your own mistakes as well as those of others, believing in God, always achieving good grades, staying true to yourself, never selling drugs or doing drugs, and always being obedient are ways to come out on top. You might assume in the city with no love to spare, that I chose the easy way out. But I didn't. I chose the road most difficult but with a better outcome.

We often think the right way is difficult to do, and that the easy way is something that comes effortlessly. However, the easy way is actually the hard way, and the hard way is really the easy way. In life, I work under the theory that it is easy to do things that are wrong in a world filled with wrong, but it is much harder to do what is right within a world filled with easy opportunities to do what is wrong. Consider this: when everyone around you is doing things the wrong way, it can become easier to fall in line with the trend. When there are kids who are living and doing things the right way that get picked on or laughed at because they're not as cool, it becomes hard to want to live that type of lifestyle. How do I know? Because I was the kid who was not as cool as everyone else until I made doing the right things cool for me and those around me. Even when I thought about switching over to the wrong or easy side, I was whooped back to reality really quickly, so I almost had no choice. There were limited times where I attempted to cross the line into the easy route. There was never a thought that crossed my mind where I thought it's funny to act out at home or in public, get bad grades, curse, or be disobedient. There was a level of responsibility placed on me from my entire community, so being defiant or testing the waters was not an option for me. There is power behind the saying, "It takes a village to raise a child." The weight of the community led me to make wiser choices and hold myself accountable for the weight of both my words and my actions. As the son of a respected man and community figurehead, the idea that my actions had to align with what I was taught became clearer. Naturally, I modeled myself after my father. My father has been the best man I have ever known, and I've always respected and valued his word like it was golden. My father had given guidance to all of his children: Westburn "Nino" Majors, Garrett "G.Money" Majors, and my right-hand man and twin, Erich "Eazy E" Majors.

Wes, the oldest of us, was the head of the crew. In my eyes, I consider Westburn the brains. He is extremely strategic, smart, thoughtful, well-mannered, and level-headed. He is the one who couldn't afford himself the opportunity to make many wrong decisions because our parents installed in him that he was to set the example for his little brothers. His window for error was very limited. As a result, he stayed on top of his grades, always modeled respect, was always responsible, and was in a position that he wanted the happiness of his brothers more than happiness for himself.

Garrett, the second oldest, is the muscle. Garrett is the original wild child with the best of both worlds. Garrett is the wild and courageous one that never let anything scare him, nor would he back down from anything or anybody. Garrett was also the one who made us all tough-minded, yet he was also extremely protective of us. He was like the ideal male Rottweiler: loving, caring, tough, and a protector. Do not get it twisted though, Garrett's grades were always on point, and he was the first one with his master's degree.

Erich is my fraternal twin brother, older by nine minutes, and a split image and character of our older brother, Westburn. Erich is an extremely strategic, patient, caring, educated, and exceptional hard worker. For the longest time, Erich and I could not be separated. We often wore the same clothes, took the same classes, played the same sports, and maintained the same thought process. We even had a period where we played tricks on our teachers and friends until they started to be able to tell us apart.

My brothers are the next most important men in my life, next to my father. Each brother provided their unique perspective on what it meant to be a man of courage, integrity, and value. What I admire most about my brothers is how much they support and believe in me, always making sure I was taken care of in all aspects of life.

Westburn always helped me with my homework whenever I needed help. He taught me how getting good grades would make mom and dad proud and how it would allow me to earn whatever I wanted. Westburn taught me the essentials of being and staying loyal to our family by any means. Westburn taught me how to believe in myself and to remember that I always had support. Garrett taught me everything concerning having a heart and being fearless in life. He taught me how to fight and would never let anybody come close to me without his permission. Garrett taught me the importance of setting goals and going to get them no matter how much adversity you have to go through to achieve them. Garrett has always been lion-hearted, and he instilled that in me. Erich was one who always just rolled with the punches with me. Sometimes, I would act and think later until I realized how I would get in trouble. He never would because he thought first and acted later, and watching that gave me a well-rounded perspective on how to handle life's situations. I always acted on instinct because I knew Erich would be there to get me out of any problem I had gotten myself into, and Erich served as my biggest fan and critic. We have gone through a lot of life situations together; learning those lessons alongside him made him my best friend. All of my siblings collectively made our father proud, and we all presented ourselves as men who sought guidance, protected family and held one another accountable in becoming better

My father was from West Chester, PA. He attended Lincoln University and became a manager of Nationwide Insurance in his prime. Most importantly, he held the title of a full-time father, provider, protector, and party man. My father would wake up at 5 am every Saturday and go to his favorite breakfast spot in the city, The Gardenia House. I will never forget it. He was there so often that every waiter or waitress and owner knew his name. By the time he sat down, his water was prepped, with extra ice to fill his water jug alongside his coffee. Since he was well known, his order would usually follow not long after his appearance

As the youngest son of four, being the baby of the crew came with both its advantages and disadvantages. I quickly had to learn how to play both sides. The biggest advantage to this was being 'too scared' to stay home with my brothers, older friends and cousins after our Friday night jammed packed sleepovers. My father and mother would always keep a good eye out on us. I always was up at the crack of dawn the next morning to meet my dad and help him tear down the massive sleeping tents we created in the living room with all of the chairs, blankets, and pillows we could find in the house. We would break down the tents and place everything at the door to head to The Gardenia House for breakfast and have our guy talks.

The Gardenia House became our special spot. It became a spot in which he would have the time and opportunity to teach me valuable life lessons, which I will get into later in the book. The Gardenia House was right around the corner from our house, and the food was amazing. I would always get the three-plate sized pancakes, eggs, bacon, orange juice, extra syrup, and sit right across from my dad at the table. It often felt like we were in some sort of exclusive business meeting. I remember it like it was yesterday. As his youngest, he always emphasized to me that an army is only as strong as the weakest link, which meant that even though I was the baby of the family, I had no free passes to be weak-minded or be held to any less of a standard than his other sons. My father was the type of father that was always extremely consistent, stood his ground, and demanded high expectations of myself and my brothers. This was especially true to anybody who stepped foot into his house and thought they were about to eat or drink anything. All of my brothers and I had to understand life's basic principles at age two, which at the time seemed like it was ridiculous. My father was famous for "The Questions" - How many letters in the alphabet? How many degrees in a circle? How many parts of speech? His most important one was when he asked us to recite the Lord's Prayer.

Anyone who has ever stepped foot into our house and was our age (sometimes even adults) knew that if you could not answer those questions, you could not eat, drink, and play a video game. Nothing would happen. He was adamant about that, along with being able to recite the Lord's Prayer by memory. Many of my friends would get it, some would be unable to answer some of the questions, and I even had a friend who studied the questions at the dining room table right after my dad asked him. Twenty-six minutes later, he went to my dad and answered all the questions. My point in describing that moment in time is to depict how, as a father, he always held us to a major standard of living. He also only wanted us around others who he could hold to the same major standard of living. He was no joke about discipline, life skills, and, most importantly, education.

Discipline wise, my father instilled a sense of fear in us that I believe every child should have in them towards their guardian. It was the type of fear that was meant to help and almost force you to do what was right. If you did not, he would make sure you never forgot it. My father was a big-time Groover, meaning he took pride in his fraternity, Groove Phi Groove. For his family and all the young men that came to his house, it seemed as though he initiated all of us into his secret fraternity, or family. He let it be known that he was in charge and that we would do as he said and not what he did. I remember as it were yesterday, he saying,

"Do what I say, not what I do." My father was no saint, but he was definitely a strong solid man and father. He was serious about us being a reflection of him. As soon as someone got out of line and sometimes, just for the heck of it, he would go get "The Wood." This was the scariest piece of wood I had ever seen in my life. We all dreaded "The Wood." It was serious! The worse was when he would give us paddles, even when we did no wrong, but just in case we even thought about it. By being my father's youngest, once again, it taught me the charisma and charm to get people on my side. As a result, I dodged plenty of paddles. There was a time he got me so good that I cringe and laugh randomly at just the mere thought of it.

Overall, that paddle taught us discipline like never before. He gave us those paddles like we were strangers, and then sat us down and made us understand exactly why we deserved them. He was a 'paddle first, ask questions, and explain later' type of father, which was extremely essential for us. As the youngest, I got to dodge so many paddles because I had learned from my older brothers', cousins' and friends' mistakes. I would hear or see them get paddled, try to hold my laughs in, then ask them why they got a paddle to never think twice about doing that to avoid that paddle. On the flip side, when my brothers, cousins, or friends received praise from our parents, aunts, or uncles, I would also ask the same question, to ensure that I was able to learn from their lessons and get the same attention from the same decisions they had made. This is a critical lesson that I'll discuss in a future chapter.

Building life skills was a big part of my father's teaching process. You see, my father never backed down or out of the role he played in our lives. He made sure that his own, and any other young men affiliated with him, understood the proper life skills to get them to mature and have an advantage over any other young men our age. Maturation as a young man was essential to him

The 'Major Preparation 11 Ways to Prepare' came from the life skills that he instilled in me since birth. As you keep reading, I will give you insight and tools that have helped me on my journey in understanding how to develop as a young man, adult, and father. My father was remarkably consistent from birth, it made our later ages a lot easier for him, and my mother was able to manage and guide us from the look in her eyes. What he would teach us, instill in us and allow us to see made me believe that Superman or Batman had nothing on my dad! One thing I always remembered him saying was, "B, as you grow and live your life, be sure to understand life's cycle. You're born, you live, and die. What you do between birth and death is up to you." My favorite line from him was, "Make sure you always get the best education possible. In this world, people can try to take everything you have, but they can never take your education."

Education-wise, my father could have sworn he was a genius. In math, it seemed like he really was a genius, but with any other subject, mom dukes had to hold us down. When I referred to my father as Superman or Batman, I was dead serious. My father was everywhere. If any of us had a game, he was present. Every event, he was in attendance. If we needed to talk, he was available, and he was there for anything we ever needed. Our father rewarded us when we did right consistently, disciplined us when we were wrong, and was so strong that he lifted all of us at the same time - two on his shoulders and two in his arms. I did not realize it then, but that picture shows how much strength, courage, passion, and determination he showed for us. I truly feel like he was just showing us how bossed up he was as a man, so we never forget that a man should always be a man, no matter the circumstances, while looking good doing it.

When I was in fourth grade, my dad challenged all of us to get all distinguished or first honors for the marking period so we could get the new Jordan sneakers. I was always pretty smart, and I knew that it would be a piece of cake for me. Long story short, report card time came, and I was the only one out of my brothers to get a C. My father did not say anything to me; he simply told us to load up the family van and took us all to New York, where my amazing mother is from and where my uncle resided as a manager of a sneaker store. When we arrived, our eyes lit up. We only ever received gifts or rewards after consistently doing the right thing. So, we parked and walked to the door, got in the store, and my dad said to get whatever Jordan's we wanted. My brothers and I darted off, but then he said, "B, where you think you're going? Come over here next to me." I tried to get into my youngest child mode, attempting to use that charm and charisma I mentioned, but heck no, it didn't work!

My brothers went to get their sneakers. Meanwhile, my mom walked away because she knew what my dad was doing and did not want to witness my reaction once I realized. A few minutes later, we were all at the register. I am steadily giving my dad the puppy eyes, trying to give him hugs, telling him that I loved him, but nothing was working. He pulled out his wallet, paid for my brothers' sneakers, and was ready to leave. My brothers took their bags, headed to the door as my dad paid the bill, and headed to the door. Lonely, I stayed at the register, looking like life was over. My dad said, "B, if you don't bring your butt on. I told you do what you had to do, and I was going to do what I was supposed to do." I cried out of the store, cried to the car, and cried in the car, trying to use my last special tricks. Needless to say, since fourth grade, I have never received anything less than a B on my report card throughout elementary or high school. My father had special ways to get through to us and make sure we understood the importance of education and how it can open opportunities for us in our lives.

My mother, on the other hand, is the queen of the earth by all means. A short, beautiful, educated, and fly lady from Brooklyn, New York. She had the look of a queen and a smile that you could never forget. She looked like she would never hurt a fly, even if she had to. I learned quickly never to let looks fool you. I truly am blessed to have her as my mother and to be her last son. As I look back and reminisce, still to this day, I do not know how my mother created so much fear, having never laid a finger on us to discipline us. Yes, our father made sure we always understood that our mother was the queen of the world, and we were never to disrespect her nor disobey her. With four boys in the home, being with her alone never prompted us to test our limits with her, even in his absence. It was that 'Brooklyn' in her eyes that we never wanted to fully witness. It was the way she carried herself. It was her demeanor. It was her style. It was the way she relentlessly and effortlessly worked so hard. It was the way she loved us all the same that demanded the utmost respect. My father was the boss of us and ran the household, but deep down, I knew my mom really ran the show at our house.

My mother, Merry Grace Majors, was extremely unique, mainly because of her upbringing, being New York raised with parents who did not take any nonsense. As my mother was growing up, she was so smart that she graduated high school early, skipping grades and ended up attending Lincoln University at 16 years old. Deep down inside, I thank and have great respect for Lincoln University for being the place to have my parents meet and become one. My mother and father stayed together, moved to Harrisburg, and began their lives together after a crazy wedding that I will allow her to get into if she ever decides to write a book about parenting (and raising boys to men).

My mother was the one who really stayed on us about education, manners, ambition, self-worth, valuing life, and becoming young men. Our mother was strict on us being well-rounded boys to men.

As I look back at our childhood, she raised four young men; young men who at one point were student-athletes, and all recipients of high school diplomas, college degrees, and master's degrees. Most importantly, she raised all four young black men, having never been a part of the judicial system. Our mother made sure extremely early that we understood to live our life. She was always willing and ready to guide us, but was very clear on one thing: if we ever end up jail, not to call her because she was not bailing us out. My mother always knew that she was giving us the jewels for how to make it in life. That was the realist thing we all heard at an extremely early age. My mother is a hero. She is the superwoman of my life. My mother is the strongest woman I know.

Mentally, she understood the process that she brought upon herself by having four boys. Not once have I ever heard or saw her complain about being a mother. I know some mothers who struggle with raising one or two children, but my mother raised, groomed, mentored, and guided four African American young men who are well mannered, educated, respectful, and goal getters.

Emotionally, my mother could have broken down many times, but not once was she ever caught slipping. Not once did she miss a sports game, miss an event, or not be there for each of us. My mother understood and accepted the fact that life was bigger than her from there on out. She always made sure we were before her. If she cooked, she made sure she ate last, or buying anything, she made sure we had what we needed first and foremost. She always went to war with or for us. She raised us never to want to embarrass her. She was extremely prideful about having us. She was at the parent-teacher meetings. She was there when we were right, to praise us, and there when we were wrong, to discipline us. What made us so proud and what took the cake for us was seeing how proud she was of us for every accomplishment, big or small. Her smile is so magnificent that it has become one of my biggest motivations ever.

I remember seeing the smile on her face after receiving my high school diploma, and when graduating from college, and her smile after my master's degree brought tears to my eyes. Her smile outweighed any and all tears. The way she would watch her work being portrayed always bought the biggest smiles on her face. My mother never questioned or altered what she stood for, what she expected out of us and made sure we were never scared of anything. She did those things by not only telling us but showing us from her actions. My mother is the true hustler of our family. She has always been so consistent with everything about life, and it rubbed off on us.

Spiritually, our mother has always been the leader in our family. Growing up, she made sure we were in church. A lot of times, we would sleep like most children, but she made sure that the spiritual foundation was instilled. My mother seasoned us spiritually just as well as she did her cooking for Sunday dinner. The start of the process of spiritual grooming was to make sure we knew she believed in her faith and that we understood our faith and religion. Having a spiritual connection was essential to her. I remember sitting in church with her on New Year's Eve 2014, listening to the sermon. It seemed like the pastor was having a direct conversation with me in front of her. Every sentence, she would look at me and smile, nudge me, or simply say, "you know God is talking to you B." Needless to say, I had the best year of my life, simply because the last year ended with my mom's smile, and the next year started with my mom's smile, a huge hug, and a conversation with God.

Physically, becoming the greatest mother in the world became second nature to her. She had a relentless sense of muscle strength and mental memory and instilled similar characteristics within all of her offspring. She gave 120% every day at life to make sure she was able to provide us with any and everything that was needed so that we had the best chances and opportunities to succeed in life. My mother never gave up at life, and she never let trials or tribulations break her. She allowed them to make her better.

My mother allowed the challenges she had to endure as motivation/ passion for life and demonstrated more love for her family. She made chasing goals and accomplishing them seem like a piece of cake. Her routine as a mother allowed her to become a guru at mothering young men. The way my mother believed in me made me believe in myself. She did a major job of preparing our family for future success.

MAJOR PREPARATION
The Process

All my life, I have been going through Major Preparation in order to prosper. Life is all about identifying and following a process and preparing for your future. Each day is the present that sets you up for your future. Your future then turns into your present, and you have to continue to strive to set up for a new future because the past becomes your history and your history makes you who you are today. I graduated from Harrisburg High - John Harris Campus in 2006. When they say high school flies by fast, it surely does. It is important to be sure that you take advantage of those years. Make sure that you build valuable relationships with friends, teachers, janitors, lunch ladies, secretaries, principals, basically any and everybody possible.

In life, you will never know who you will need or who can help you reach your next level of living. Understand that the friends you have may be courageous enough to become the world's greatest president, doctor, firefighter, author, lawyer, dentist, sports star, etc.

Realize that the teachers are there to help guide you - not see you fail. Teachers are major assets to the world, but they do not receive the credit they deserve, but you can display to them the appreciation and credit they do deserve. Teachers are in school to help you build your character and put you through major preparation academically, socially, and mentally in order to prepare you for the next chapter of life.

In life, you never know what someone has to offer, so even though many overlook janitors in school, they usually have some of the best wisdom the world can offer. If you sit down and have a conversation with a school janitor, you would be amazed at their wisdom and thought process. The lunch ladies back in my time were the moms at school, and if you were on their side, they made sure when they saw your smile, they hooked your plate up. Secretaries can make sure you are always on point. They can vouch for you, and most importantly, they are so loving and genuinely care about your ultimate well-being. Principals are often looked at as the bad guys, mainly because students force them to administer the disciplinary processes by deciding to go through high school the hard way vs. the easy way (following the rules). Principals can be a valuable resource for advice and recommendations. In high school, your support system will be the largest and most consistent it may ever be in life. Adults in schools are there because they have a calling to be there or genuinely have students' best interests in mind.

Many students feel that they will not need anybody and that they are big and bad until graduation time comes and then reflect on all the bridges they burned. See, I was the one who took advantage of the wisdom and guidance of others. Life is so much easier when we learn from the successes and mistakes of others. I did not fight against the authority in school. I was on their side, which ultimately came with great memories. I eventually graduated with a 3.9 GPA, was a starting point guard for the Harrisburg Cougars for two years, a scholar in The School of Business and Industry Program, The Gentleman's Club, and had extreme support because I applied myself the best that I could. Playing basketball for the Harrisburg Cougars was a roller coaster ride, and it put me through life situations that prepared me for real-world experiences.

COLLEGE EXPERIENCE

I graduated from Susquehanna University in 2010 with a 3.6 GPA. I became the first African American male to earn a degree in elementary education. In addition to academic success, I had an outstanding basketball career – earning recognition as Rookie of the Year, two-time conference Defensive Player of the Year, the career leader in assists, second leader in steals, two-year captain and four-year starter. The story of how Susquehanna came about was fantastic and happened based on the charisma and charm my father taught me.

A man named Dave Brown, who was then a basketball coach at Susquehanna University, saw me playing at a Five-Star basketball camp during the summer of 2005. From there, history was in the making. He called the head coach on the spot and became a mentor for the rest of my collegiate experience. It was so funny because I was being recruited from a variety of colleges, and Dave Brown seemed like the only one who truly and sincerely cared for my well-being as a city kid from Harrisburg. A few weeks later, the entire coaching staff showed up at my house in

Harrisburg, sat at the dining room table to talk to my family and me about attending their university. As soon as the coaches got there, the first words out of my mouth were, "What is up with the football team and coach? My twin brother is the man on the field. If you want me, you want him. We are a package deal." They then looked at my mom and dad and could do nothing but laugh because I thought I was calling all the shots. I ran down all of the guidelines and requirements for me to attend their school, and they asked, "Is that it?" In an attitude that said, if that's the case, you might as well sign the papers right now.

I told them how I needed the fair shot to take the point guard's spot. I needed the jersey number 11. I needed to be roommates with my brother, we needed the best financial package possible, and lastly, my mom and dad needed VIP parking to every football and basketball game. One lesson my father taught me was that in life, you must ask for whatever you want and the worst someone can say is 'No,' but they can always say yes.

Everything was in line and all requests were granted. Coming from a predominately African American high school to a predominately white university was somewhat shocking to me. Going to Susquehanna University taught me about diversity and how to function with all races.

I took the same theories and methods to Susquehanna University in regard to life and networking. I eventually met my college best friend and basketball running mate, Marcus Burke (a famous writer today, and we still talk daily). My college coach, Frank Marcinek, was one of the best coaches I ever had due to his will to win at life even more than basketball. Coach Marcinek and I were perfect matches for each other. Both were strong-minded and wanted to win no matter what it took. It was also an amazing feeling knowing that the university staff from the President, Jay Lemons, all the way down to the famous lunch lady, Momma Donna, loved everything about what I stood for as a student-athlete. One special woman who believed in me from the very first day I met her was my favorite professor, MJ Fair. She was the mother away from home, and I am not over exaggerating. She believed in me so much that there was no way I was going to let her down. She made me feel so much at ease about life and groomed me to become the first African American male to graduate from the elementary education department. She understood everything I was going through, and if she did not, she would at least listen. In life, people who believe in you will invest everything they have in you as long as you receive the information and love they want to share with you. Wait until I tell you about the experiences at Susquehanna University!

I then attended Penn State University – Harrisburg Campus, where my mother, Westburn, Erich, and I all attended and earned our Master of Public Administration degrees. While attending Penn State, I was a graduate assistant with the basketball team and worked as an assistant to the athletic director. The mentorship and guidance I received from Rahsaan Carlton, the Athletic Director, was unbelievable.

While attending Penn State-Harrisburg Campus, I began laying the foundation for Major Preparation based on life lessons taught by my father about always being prepared for life's opportunities and challenges. I developed the organization with the mission to help others – particularly youth and young adults - to be prepared to address individual obstacles that undermine the achievement of life goals. Major Preparation is focused on strategies to effectively identify and address each individual's needs by promoting a positive self-image, establishing a strong work ethic, and general healthy lifestyle across all ages and demographics. Through motivational speaking, personal fitness, basketball training and an urban clothing line, Major Preparation reaches out to people to reinforce the importance of respect for themselves and others. It reinforces the establishment of personal goals and objectives, to focus on Educational and Athletic excellence, and most importantly, to break the cycle of mediocrity and shoot to #BeMajor!

Get ready for this roller coaster ride. I am going to take you through how essential going through Major Preparation is as youths and adults to maximize your life. I will go in-depth on a lot of life-changing experiences that will blow your mind but will also encourage you to take pride in your life and your preparation process to reach your goals.

The Foundation
Chapter 1:

PREPARE TO MAKE GOALS BECOME REALITY:

"You Can Do All Things Through Christ Who Strengthens You"
Phil: 4-13.

Prepare to make goals become a reality. In life, there is a false sense of what really matters. Many will say that cars, clothes, money, and jewelry are what matters most. In all actuality, what should matter the most is God, family, education, and goals. Growing up in the church helped me to create this theory. When I was young, our family was in the church faithfully. The church not only educates you on your religion but also slows life down in general. Too often, people fly through life without taking the time to see and accept their blessings that are received daily. You have to appreciate and be thankful for all blessings that you receive, small or large. As you grow through life, you must understand that God's job is to take you through the Major Preparation process to see if you have what it takes to prosper. When you can wake up, have clothes on your back, have feet to walk on, have the ability to speak, eyes to see, a roof over your head, food to eat, or water to drink, you are considered blessed.

CHILD OF GOD

By being a child of God, it is a fact that if you keep pushing yourself, you will keep getting better! At certain times in life, you are flat out going to get your butt whipped, and your teeth kicked in along your journey. It is inevitable. You will get hit in the mouth. You will then realize that if it does not kill you, it really was not that bad in the first place. You are fully capable of getting up and fighting the good fight of life. You already have the characteristics embedded within you to achieve your goals. Your life must mean more to you than it means to others. One thing about life is that it goes on - with or without you. It continues, so taking control and pride in your life, decision-making skills, and determination to accomplish your goals is essential. Throughout life, you will see that there is enough room for everyone to #BeMajor. Even though many may have similar goals, we all have our unique characteristics that make our goals different. Too often, many get caught up on what someone else is doing instead of staying locked in on making your goals become a reality. We often will take another person's major accomplishments and compare them to our own. This can make you feel as if your major work is not bringing in the same major results. However, you must remain focused on your goal to get your own results.

The Major Preparation motto is "Putting in Major Work for Major Results," which pertains to all aspects of life. No matter if you want to be a doctor, lawyer, police officer, nurse, fireman, athlete, teacher, astronaut, pediatrician, or entrepreneur, you have to put in the work to get the results. Before you turn your goals into reality, it is essential that you create a list of goals, create a vision board, create guidelines for yourself to force your hand, and test your abilities. When I was a kid, my grandfather always asked me what I wanted to be when I grew up. I would always answer, "I want to be like my dad, Pop-Pop." Then he would explain that my father is the ideal father for me to want to emulate, but emphasized the importance of a profession or craft. My grandfather always told me to never want to become like someone but to always strive to be better than that person by working harder than him or her.

As I grew older, my grandfather helped me to create a list of goals that I would want to obtain throughout my lifetime. Having that list of goals helped guide my actions throughout my childhood. A majority of the time, I would always be on point because I understood that I had a variety of tasks that needed to be accomplished, and my focus was on completing the tasks at hand in order to move and shift into the other goals set before me. Having goals allows you to hold yourself accountable for your actions. Ever since I was in the sixth grade, I understood the importance of goals. I always had them hung up in my bedroom near my door so that I had to see and read them every day. As you grow and mature in life, you can never be *too* focused, and you can never read your goals *too* much.

Through life's experience, you will realize that you have to strive and work through smaller accomplishments at the start. As you look back, you will realize you have more strength and capability now to make it than you may have thought in the beginning. Once I got to college, my goal list transferred to weekly checklists with the ultimate semester goals in mind. Every day, I had a checklist of what I needed to accomplish with the understanding that if I just master the day, then the semester will become extremely easy. At the end of my first semester in college, I made the Dean's List. When I told my mom what I did, she asked me, "B, how did you do that? I knew you were smart, but not too many freshmen make Deans List." I replied, "You know, momma ain't raise no fool!" She laughed, and I could see her smile through the phone. That moment was an indicator that there were no obstacles to becoming major that I couldn't overcome, as long as I remained focused on the end goal.

PERSONAL RELATIONSHIP WITH GOD

Having goals will become the basis from which you will develop a sense of who you truly are on earth pertaining to the essential aspects of life. Your first goal should be focused on your natural obligation to God. When I was younger, maybe around eight or nine years old, I didn't understand the importance of having a relationship with God even though I grew up in the church. I was mainly going because I had no choice. My parents guided the process that I had to go through spiritually before I completely crossed over and had the urge to get baptized. I then learned that my relationship with God was more important than any relationship with anyone on earth. I gave in to God's plan for my life as opposed to my own plan. My spiritual goals were to say the Lord's Prayer every night and every morning and read five verses of the Bible a day while going to church every Sunday.

Staying in line with those few goals gave me the edge I needed from God - to believe in Him, in my parents and myself. My goals worked for me, and they became second nature, mental memory, and guided my upbringing. I had friends who did not grow up in the church nor had an obligation to God. Looking back, the separation is clear, and I had an extreme advantage in everything that I did because of my relationship with God.

Creating spiritual goals helps guide and manifest your other goals. Below, write five spiritual goals that you can commit to. After you write them here, write them on a separate sheet of paper as well. Place the list next to your bed so that you can see it every morning that you're blessed enough to open your eyes and every night before you lay your eyes to rest. Utilize this activity as a way to remain grounded in your spiritual guidance, which ultimately helps to drive your motivation with other goals.

MY SPIRITUAL GOALS

1. _____
   _____

2. _____
   _____

3. _____
   _____

4. _____
   _____

5. _____
   _____

Now that you have your goals down, hold yourself accountable, and stick to them. Your relationship with God is the most important relationship you can have. I have grown never to question God. The world has a duty to test our faith in Him. God will forgive your every mistake and every sin because that is what He does. As long as we are on earth, it is almost impossible never to make a mistake or commit a sin, which is disrespectful to God. However, despite that reality, He forgives, and a part of that forgiving process is in us never forgetting that He allows us that mercy. As you go through life, understand that you will be tested, and if you are truly committed and faithful to Him, you will be blessed. Even more importantly, your family will be blessed!

FAMILY GOALS

As your relationship goals with God grows, you will grow, and your family will continue to love and believe in you. They will help you strive towards your goals. Family is supposed to be forever. Love from family can grow to be unconditional, and showing love to your family members must be the first family goal. When you have family love and support, it catapults you into becoming extremely confident. Believe me when I say with God's love and your family's love, you will feel like nothing in the world can stop you. With family, the ultimate goal should be to hold that next family member to the highest standard of living possible. Being blessed with family must mean that life is about more than just you. Whether you like it or not, you are a reflection of your family. The decisions you make, the grades you get, the language you use, the way you present yourself in public or at school, and, most importantly, your respect levels are all vital reflections of your family. You may or may not be receiving the most love from your family, but you have the capability to show the most love even at a young age. If you are not receiving as much love, it may make you feel less self-confident, but best believe that God knows what you are going through, and He will always show you the exact amount of love that you need to rise at that time in your life.

Now, if you are fortunate enough to be one who receives unconditional love from your family, do not take it for granted. Soak in every ounce of love that they give you. The amount of love received can even be enough to share with those around you who may not have the same level of love that you have.

In my eyes, when it comes to family, there are two types of love; unconditional love and tough love. Unconditional love is just what was explained. It's holding your family members to the highest standard of living possible and loving each other no matter what happens. If everyone in a family holds one another to the highest standard of living possible, the foundation for the family will become so solid that the family's reputation will be extremely prestigious. Having that unconditional love is flat out taking pride in your first, and definitely your last name and not letting it down.

Now, tough love is where some get it confused. Tough love is when family members never sugar coat anything. When you receive tough love, you will not understand what is happening in the first few times. But once you get a chance to reflect on what happened, you will understand every bit of it. When receiving that tough love, understand that the person giving it to you usually has your best interest in mind. In receiving that tough love, you will be told things you will not want to hear. You will get punishments you will not want, and you will get the discipline that you feel is not fair. Best believe, when you grow up, you will understand and be thankful for that tough love. Tough love is not meant to intentionally hurt you but rather humble you into knowing that you have to live up to God's standard and your family's standard of living.

In my family, love is truly unconditional, which for us has always been that way. I was fortunate to have both parents in my life for twenty years, so they set the standard for our family. My brothers and I would run through a brick wall to express our love for the family if needed. Many outsiders won't believe the unconditional and tough love we portray as brothers because it is so uncommon. We are each other's biggest fans and also our toughest critics. We will praise each other throughout every accomplishment, but at the drop of a dime, we would show that tough love to one another if we were acting in a manner that lessens or disrespects the family's name and reputation. As the youngest, my brothers all had their ways of showing love to me. Westburn would always show so much unconditional love that I never wanted to disappoint him. Garrett showed so much tough love to my twin brother that I never wanted to get him to show me that level of tough love. My twin, Erich, and I have been through so much in life together that we had to show both unconditional and tough love to each other so that we always stayed on point.

With family, love builds family loyalty. Our family's second goal was always to be loyal to the name 'Majors.' I have the acronym F.O.R.G tattooed on my arm, which stands for 'Family's Our Reliable Guidance.' Garrett taught me that acronym and told me to always make sure I live by it. Having loyalty is so critical, especially in a world of so many people who will cross you at their convenience. Being loyal does not mean being one who has to do everything someone says without question. Being loyal is being there when needed by remembering how many times someone was there for you, not recounting the times they might not have been.

Loyalty has become a lost characteristic, but when your family love and bond is truly tight, it can never be broken. Families do grow apart at times, but the loyalty and love should never go astray. In this life, a family is not only the ones that share your last name, but those who share trying times, childhood memories, and lonely nights when you need that shoulder to cry on or a person who was there when you needed them. When family members do grow apart, you sometimes have to let them go and grow on their own in order to come back to the family.

I had a friend who was as close to me as any blood relative. We did practically everything together. He was a big-time track athlete, football player, and inspiring rap artist. He was a year older than I was. During high school, our bond got weak due to life in general. As we grew older, we always had love and loyalty to one another, but the bond was just not the same. Instead of us talking it out and getting back on track, we went years without talking, and then he passed away due to a terrible accident. It hurt so bad seeing him go, not only because he was family, but because the time apart could have been mended and he may not have been in the situation he was in had we remained close. He was at my house all the time, and I was at his. Some of my first nights ever in the heart of a rough neighborhood were spent with him. He was truly a brother to me who I never lost love or loyalty towards, although the egos got in the way of our reconciliation.

With my own brothers, there is no way for us ever to fall apart (mainly because Westburn is never allowing it) because our father always made sure that we knew if all else failed, we were still all that we had. The loyalty between us runs blood vessels deep. There was a point in life when my father decided that he was going to yell at our mom while we were home. It may not have been the very first time, but we were fed up with him raising his voice at her. We basically 'cliqued up' in Wes's room and formed our own army, with Wes leading the way, Garrett being the muscle, following up with Erich and me into our father's room. We walked in and stated, "We are tired of hearing you raising your voice at our mom. If it happens again, you have to deal with all of us." At that point, all he could say was, "No problem, fellas. I will not do it again." The moment he realized he was wrong, he also realized that he groomed sons who would always stay loyal to each other and their mom. He then also realized he could not take on all of us, so needless to say, we never heard him raise his voice at her again. From that moment on, I knew that as long as we stuck together, we could conquer the world. So, loyalty runs deep, and knowing that you have a loyal family is a major confidence booster.

So far, we've covered love and loyalty; all that is left is respect.

Family respect has a direct correlation with love and loyalty. Respecting your family is a goal that can never be taken lightly. Respect towards family is something in which we all took pride. Respect has always been vital because of the family's legacy. You see, our family roots are from West Chester, PA, New York and Panama. Our past family members put in a great deal of work for my parents, brothers, and me to be a part of this family. We understood that we had to honor and continue to live with a great deal of respect for our last name, Majors, which is my father's side, and Samuel, my mother's side of the family.

Another important part of that family respect level is in our sense of privacy. My family and I would sit at our dinner table Sunday nights and have conversations about life that would lead my father to state, "What is said at the table, stays at the table." This meant that everything our family talked about was not meant for anyone else to know, which included other aunts, uncles, cousins, family members, or friends. Both of our parents taught us different things at the dinner table that I still use today. At our dinner table, no televisions were on, and no cell phones were allowed. Our only focus was to eat, be attentive, and have direct dialogue with family. My parents taught us important lessons at that table such as no elbows on the table, always saying your prayers before eating, chewing with your mouth closed, not talking with a mouth full of food, not interrupting someone else while they are talking, and, most importantly, how to have eye contact, comprehend and show respect when listening to others.

What are your family goals? What can, or should be your family goals? Write five in the book; then, write them on the same sheet of paper as your spiritual goals.

FAMILY GOALS

1. _____

_____

2. _____

_____

3. _____

_____

4. _____

_____

5. _____

_____

Having Sunday dinners is one of my best childhood memories ever. We had assigned seats at the dinner table. My mom and dad stayed at the head of the table. I stayed next to my mom on her right side, while Erich would be next to me on my right side. Garrett stayed across from me, and Westburn was across from Erich. Those memories were not only about life lessons but also about fellowshipping and building the family's foundation. Now don't get me wrong; all of the life lessons were amazing. I greatly appreciate them all. What was equally mesmerizing was that my mom would throw down in that kitchen every Sunday like it was Thanksgiving. My mother always made sure we ate well. I still do not know why she fed a grown man and her four boys every single Sunday, like it would be the last meal we would ever eat. My mother worked so hard without boasting about what she did. She just walked around, making the world look so easy to live in, which I appreciated.

I used to love when she made breakfast for dinner because when she didn't, she would always make me eat vegetables. Her breakfast for dinner meals I had to eat last because I was like the garbage man, whatever everyone else did not eat, I ate for sure. When she would make regular dinners of fried chicken, mac and cheese, butter rolls, rice, string beans, cabbage, etc., I was a fan of everything but vegetables. It got so bad that she would have to make my plate, ensuring that she added vegetables to it. I would be forced to eat my vegetables, and after a while, I learned a super dope trick from using my imagination. I would smile as my mom made my plate, eat all of the food (even ask for more), tell my mom how amazing everything was, but put the vegetables in my mouth, and hold them up in my cheeks. After, I would ask to use the bathroom and spit them all out. I got away with it for a while. That is until I told one of my brothers, who eventually told my mom on me when I got on their nerves. From then on, I had to eat my vegetables first before anything.

Once again, I got creative. I'd put my vegetables in my mouth then take a huge gulp of water so that I could swallow them instead of eating them. I eventually got caught after my dad caught on to what I was doing and whooped my butt with "The Wood" for wasting my food and not being appreciative of my dinner. Eventually, I gave into the process of having to eat vegetables after I was out of options. My brothers laughed and laughed and would always remind me about me trying to be slick rather than doing the right thing.

Those Sunday dinners not only established our family goals, but they instilled real-life lessons and applications within our fellowship that helped prepare me to endure the major life journey I had ahead of me. Each Sunday dinner served a purpose of fellowship, but that table also served as an important learning environment.

PREPARE TO ENDURE THE MAJOR PREP LIFE JOURNEY

In life, you are born with a blank slate. Everything you learn comes mainly from what you see and hear. Your outlook on life is shaped based on what you have been taught or were allowed to see/experience. Too often in life, youth get blamed for negative actions and are rarely praised for positive actions. See, youth with negative actions and views did not wake up all of a sudden having those views. Someone exposed them to those types of negative views. Someone may not have shown them the unconditional love, attention, praise, guidance, structure, and life lessons that they deserve. Consequently, they will still get blamed for their negative actions. Parents have to be held more accountable for shaping children's positive behaviors and productive goal setting for life.

No one can ask to come into this world at any time. When someone is brought into the world, it is essential that they get the love, guidance, structure, and attention that they deserve, so he or she has a foundation and becomes prepared to endure the major life journey.

On the flip side, when a child is on point, respectful, has goals, great grades, and only positive vibes, the parents get all the credit right away.

This comparison is essential to point out because one scenario acknowledges the impact of parental guidance while the other omits it. Parents and guardians spend the most time spent with a child, and if the parent wants all the praise for a good child, then parents should be held accountable for negative behavior and thought processes taught to the child as well.

One of the first lessons I learned that helped me prepare for life's journey was not letting anyone steal my goals. I took heed to the possibility that all my goals could come true. One thing that I've realized is that your goals are going to be your goals, regardless of who likes them or not. My goals helped me to believe I could become unstoppable, uncommon, and a rare breed in life because I was not scared to be different. I understood that nothing was going to be easy to accomplish. I realized that I would get knocked down often in life, but as long as I had goals, I would have a reason to get up. I learned that anything worth having in life was worth fighting for. I learned that I had to go after my goals with all that I had in me. I learned that as long as I knocked down daily goals, my ultimate goals would become easier. I learned that there would be those who do not believe in you because they are not you. I learned that as long as I was chasing my goals that I would do better than good and better than most because of the mentality that was instilled in me. I learned that having a positive outlook mixed with a great deal of faith would have a great impact on my life.

When I was in the ninth grade, I came up with an addition problem: Positive Thought + Positive Actions = Positive Outcomes. I thought of that problem and ran with it for the rest of my life. My goals from fourth grade to twelfth grade, an eight-year span, were to get first or distinguished honors every marking period. Also, to get my chores done every week, do my pushups and sit-ups every day, never disappoint my parents, work my hardest in every sport (especially basketball), stay away from drugs and graduate from high school.

My goals were all extremely realistic. I accomplished them, and they are giving me the structure for the way I am living my life and the way people think of me. I created smaller goals that shaped my character.

Those smaller goals made it easier to establish my relationships with others who understood my work ethic and knew that in accomplishing the smaller goals, I was prepping myself for the larger goals ahead of me.

What are your personal goals for the next eight years? Write them below, and then transfer them to the same sheet as your spiritual and family goals.

PERSONAL GOALS

1. _____
   _____

2. _____
   _____

3. _____
   _____

4. _____
   _____

5. _____
   _____

As I walked through life, I had to realize that my attitude would help me endure many of life's roadblocks. Your attitude is a direct reflection of who you are. Your attitude can make or break who you are and how others view you. The only way for you to face your attitude problems or to continue to have a positive attitude is to stand up to yourself. Too often, people forget that you have to be able to look yourself in the mirror and be happy about who you are and what you represent. It is often more difficult to face yourself than to confront others around you. Throughout my life, my attitude was not always the greatest, but I learned to adjust because the ones who were in my life left me with no choice. They expected me to check my attitude and place my best foot forward with a positive attitude. In my younger years, my excuse for my bad attitude was that I was the youngest child, and I was entitled to have what I wanted. I was redirected so fast that I had no choice but to understand that I was entitled to what I consistently worked for, and not merely what I wanted. There was an expectation to work for what I wanted, and that shifted my attitude in a way that allowed me to understand the value of working for what I wanted, rather than simply expecting anything because of who I was.

In order to endure the major life journey, I had to develop the habit of doing more than what was asked of me. Not only so that I could be in the good graces of others, but so that I understood that in order to separate myself from others, I had to outwork them. When I was young, my parents gave us all chores on certain days. I used to complete just enough to make the minimum allowance. After a while, I noticed my brother, Wes, made more money than I did. I eventually asked him how he made more than me, and he simply said, "Because I work harder than you B. I have a lot more to do." He may not even realize this, but after that, I began to want to do my chores. I began to ask my brothers to do their chores if they would give me some of their allowance. That simple scenario let me know even then that I had to work harder to get more. I took that lesson on and carried that mindset into every aspect of my life.

My work ethic grew so strong because of the way I saw people around me work. My parents put in work, my uncles put in work, my brothers put in work, my friends put in work, and even my idol, NBA point guard, Allen Iverson, put in work. I did not know Allen Iverson, but I watched and studied his game so much that I felt like I knew him personally. I was so fascinated with his abilities and how hard he worked. I looked at him as somebody I could be if I worked hard enough. My father once told me, "If you put the work in now, later, you will be just fine." I grew to work so hard at home, at school, and in sports, because I wanted to outwork everybody in the world. I worked so hard that I never got tired. Even in grade school, I knew that I had to push myself. The spirit in me never allowed me to not work hard at my goals so I could become who I was destined to be. I made up my mind that I was going to do nothing but win at life. I was hungry at life and wanted to endure whatever it took to become successful. I just wanted to show the world that Bryan Majors was going to be legendary because I was not afraid to live my purpose.

The biggest lesson I came to understand about life was that no one gets out of life alive. I had to understand that throughout life, you have to keep your priorities intact and find a balance of enjoyment because there is a beginning and an end to every process. I became one who would keep my priorities first, and then my secondary priority became to make others smile, laugh, and have a great time in my presence. I was blessed enough to have a solid upbringing but was taught that more blessings come to you as you become a blessing to others. Life taught me that I could never let anyone steal my goals, that I must have a great attitude, be willing to go above and beyond, and have a major work ethic.

As you think about your life's journey, write down five different ways you can endure life's journey.

WAYS TO ENDURE LIFE'S JOURNEY

1. _____
   _____
2. _____
   _____
3. _____
   _____
4. _____
   _____
5. _____
   _____

While having the courage to endure life's process and going after your goals, understand that distractions are a part of the process. Distractions are necessary while enduring life's process because they test your self-discipline and focus. If you want to ensure your goals become a reality, you have to maintain your focus. There are a multitude of distractions that try to get in your way. These distractions can come most often from family, friends, and even the streets.

LIVING LIFE COURAGEOUSLY

When you are living life courageously, as one willing to conquer the world, not afraid of failure, willing to act right in a world of wrong, and one who hates mediocrity and thrives to **#BeMajor**, you will find that many will not want to see you succeed. They will envy your implementation of the determination, drive, courage, work ethic, motivation, and self-discipline that we all have, but that you decided to apply in your life. Family can be a distraction if they do not keep you humbled. Family members should never let one person become bigger than the family. Some family members will be so fascinated by your work ethic and see your potential that they will ride your wave instead of creating their own wave to ride. Some family members will distract you by wanting you to do what is best for them versus what will be best for you, stopping you from peaking and working on your craft. Family can sometimes be the biggest distraction because they spend the most time with you as you go through your maturation process. Friends can become a distraction if you are not friends with like-minded people.

The street life distraction is a level all on its own. The streets give off one of the greatest senses of false hope you can ever think of in life. The streets provide a false sense of love, care, loyalty, trust, honor, and respect that many would do anything to have. This is especially true if those elements are not being given at home. I have some friends, cousins and old heads that were incredible leaders and athletes, but got distracted by the streets. Some of their stories have really impacted my life. These people are friends and family, and were really knee-deep in the game.

The first story is about a guy who was one of the best football players in his grade level and the entire area for a while before the streets distracted him. He was from an area where you either played sports or sold drugs. He only got into the streets because his mother passed away when he was a teenager, his father and brother were both in jail, leaving just him and his sisters behind. His sisters struggled to try to provide for them. At the age of sixteen, he decided that he no longer wanted to see them struggle, so he jumped to the streets. He was determined to either get money to provide for them, go to jail, or die trying. That was the culture of where he was from, so he believed it was the only option. Overall, he was tired of not having anything! He thought his "out" was going to be making it into the NFL. However, when his mother died, he had to support his family, the only way he knew how. That caused him to turn to the streets and give up on his goals to survive and become the provider for the family.

From the outside looking in, it looked like he was beginning to have it all. He had all of the money, cars, clothes, the best chains, girls, and respect. You name it, and he had it. But what many did not know was that he had a family, friends, and a hood for which he was responsible. He had to take care of so many people, and with that came respect. He never had to look over his shoulder to protect what he had. The only way his money was going to be taken from him was if the Feds caught him. Never did he fear someone robbing him. What was crazy about him was that he was in the streets, but that did not interfere with the type of person he was outside of the streets. Do not get it twisted; he had to stand for what he represented in the streets when he was in the streets. When he was not in the streets, he was a whole different person. He had the respect of everyone in the city. Everyone showed him love. Everybody wanted to be connected to him because he was a real boss, in and out of the streets.

I remember a time he picked me up one day when I was a senior in high school. He pulled up in his truck with huge rims on it. I was scared as hell to get in his truck because I knew who he was and what type of lifestyle he had.

Sensing my hesitation, he told me, "B, I do not have any drugs or money in my truck. I just want to talk to you." I then got in his truck, and we rode around the city. He let me wear his iced out chain while he was dropping jewels on me about life. The most important line he dropped on me was, "B, you have what it takes. This street life is not all it appears to be. Whatever you may need, do not go to the streets looking for it. Come to me first. Keep playing ball and getting good grades."

Hearing those words from him at that time boosted my confidence to sky high. The biggest drug dealer had just picked me up, not to put drugs on my lap but to tell me to stay away from the streets. I eventually held him to his word, and when prom time came around, I asked to take his truck to the prom, and of course, he kept his word. I pulled up to the prom in the hottest car in the city with 24-inch rims, banging the song 'Number One Stunner.'

What I appreciated about him was that he saw how the streets distracted him from who he could have been but did not want them to distract me. He was truly brilliant, never touching the drugs, always keeping a job, and staying away from drinking or doing drugs his entire life. He kept a clear mind, which allowed him to always be attentive in the life he was living. He eventually hit a roadblock when he was at the playground with his kids. They were three years old, and he was watching them play, seeing the enjoyment and excitement in their eyes and knowing they had no worries in the world. At that moment, he realized that if he continued down the path he was on, he would eventually get caught, and his kids would have to grow up the same way he did - in poverty, without food, clothes - and in the same environment in which he grew up. He loved where he came from because everyone was family. They had all played sports together, and there was genuine love, but not what he wanted his children to have to endure.

When he left the streets, the streets were not the same for a while until there became a new boss. News that he left the streets was bigger than any news on television, but he had to refocus on God, his children, and being alive. Needless to say, today, he is one of few who got out alive and away from jail. He was such a boss that he went from boss on the streets to a boss in the corporate world, a boss father, and a boss in the community with youth sports all within a year of being away from the street. At this point, the love, respect, care, loyalty, honor, and trust from the street guys did not matter to him because he switched his priorities. He still receives that same love, respect, care, loyalty, honor, and trust from his family, which matters the most. He also has his friends, who respected his decision to leave the streets and now live in the corporate world. Looking at his example, you may feel that his situation is unique. His decision to turn his life around for the better is one that any person can make. While the scenario may seem one of a kind, we can all decide to turn away from our poor decision and create new and better choices.

On the flip side, there is another guy who was all about the street life. I did not know him personally, but everybody in the city knew of him because of who he was in the streets. Everything about him looked like money. He was a walking dollar sign for sure. From the outside looking in, it looked so appealing that it was crazy. He was the man in the streets in a time where authentic jerseys were in style. He had a jersey for every day of the year with jewelry, sneakers, and hats to match every jersey. Any room he walked in, you could tell he had big-time money. His charisma, his walk, his demeanor all represented that he was getting it. Seeing him carry himself the way he did was amazing to me. What I did not realize is that I had those same characteristics and following. I did not realize that I did because my money, car, and jewelry did not match his. I gained his respect by being the star high school basketball player and not being in the streets, so we would speak but never had direct experiences with one another.

It was crazy with him because he was here one minute and gone the next. It went from everybody talking about him to nobody saying anything else about him in the snap of a finger. I remember having a conversation with one of my friends about him and where he was, and they replied, "He is not the man anymore. He is locked up. He has some serious time, so it's on to the next boss." It was years since I last saw him. When I had the chance to speak to him again, the connection was unreal. I told him how seeing his life helped me make certain decisions for my life. He is another person who fell victim to the streets and only had to do jail time. Since he has been home, he completely changed his life around. His priorities went from money, car, clothes, and jewelry to God, family, and goals. It is a blessing because he is alive today and was willing to bless me with some words of wisdom, some of which are in this book to help impact your life.

This next story is extremely sensitive to me because it is about a friend of mine who was like a brother. My mom and dad loved him like he was their own. He was at my house every weekend. We played youth football with the East Shore Royals together. He was short, fast, strong, and not scared of anyone. He played running back and had moves like Barry Sanders, one of his idols back then. He was the hardest person to try and tackle because he was so elusive. On the baseball field, he played every position, could hit that ball, and always made big plays. He came from a good family with support and love, but as we continued to grow up, he became a product of the company he kept versus the company he once knew. I could have sworn that he was going to make it in football or baseball and use his gifts as his ticket to stardom, to get his family out of Harrisburg, and to prove to the world that he had what it took to **#BeMajor**.

I began to feel the distance that he was creating between us around our freshman year in high school, although I did not understand why. Months went by when he and I did not talk or see each other, but I did not think much of it. Then I ran into him months later at a local youth party. Although he was so happy to see me, I could tell that he was completely different than before when he and I were real close friends. I remember like it was yesterday. His pants were sagging real low; he had a chain on, hat backward, and was not the person who was once like a brother to me. I asked him, "What is good, bro? I miss you, man. Why don't you come by anymore?" All he could do over the music was give a hug, dap me up and say, "Bro, some things done changed, I have to get this money but tell mom, dad and the brothers I love 'em." Then he looked me the eyes and walked away. From there on, I knew my friend was hooked to the streets with no return at that time.

I would see him with a crew of street guys, and it confirmed my assumptions. It was confirmation that all of his talents were poured down the drain. The street pressure of getting money, cars, clothes, jewelry stripped the potential NFL and MLB star from his talents. He eventually got jammed up for drugs and was sentenced to years in jail. I always stayed in contact with him, and guess what? He may be home by the time this book drops, but the words that he was sharing with me to create this aspect of the book are words from him while incarcerated in 2015, after years of being away from his family, friends, and child.

When I tell you the streets have no true love, respect, or honor, trust and believe it. Some get lucky enough to live a street life and make tons of money, but the majority never make it out, get gunned down, snitched on, lose friends or family, get robbed, fear for their own life, lose everything they have and have people's backs turned on them as soon as they cannot provide. The streets are not worth the risk, although they get so much praise. So, it is essential that you keep and surround yourself with those who will hold you to a major standard of living and not let distractions overtake you.

Distractions hinder your progress. Here, you will identify that distractions can prevent you from reaching your goals. After you create your list, realize that now you can visualize what your distractions possibly are and not allow them to dictate your life. Write your list here and on the same sheet as your spiritual, family, and personal goals to further identify ways to endure life's journey.

DISTRACTIONS

1. _____

2. _____

3. _____

4. _____

5. _____

BUILD YOUR TEAM

In life, you become a product of the company you keep. So you must take pride in building your team. If you decide to have friends who are about that street life, then there is a great chance of falling victim to the streets. If you want to have friends who all want to be entrepreneurs, artists, doctors, lawyers, nurses, cops, athletes, coaches, agents, trainers, etc., then you will more than likely fall in line with that as well. It is crucial who your parents and family are and who they allow you to be around because it is going to determine what type of company you decide to affiliate with in your life. Again, when we are born, we are all born with a blank slate, so you become a product of what you see, hear, learn, and expose yourself to in your environment.

I am fortunate because my 'team' was based on friends who all came from similar backgrounds. As the youngest, they all had an obligation to make sure I was prepared for life. They were not only capable of telling me which direction to go, but they were also able to lead by example. We were blessed with mothers and fathers, decent homes, and born into a solid foundation where at any point, we could have gone astray but chose otherwise. The foundation that I was born into was a crew called St. Paul Warriors. Being four years younger than Westburn allowed me to not only be affiliated with my friends but his as well. His crew became my old heads, so I knew that although I was too young to run with them, they were there for me if I ever needed anything from them. Garrett is only two years older than me, so his crew really rubbed off on Erich and me. We became like the last of the crew for a while. I mean, we rolled deep, and some eventually grew apart, going their separate ways.

We eventually became a group of young men called "The Good Fellas," a crew founded on loyalty, trust, and respect. We were a group of guys and our secret weapon named Cece, who we affectionately called "the First Lady."

Cece was an important member of our circle as the only female in 'Good Fellas.' She was the only female that we became protective of her like we had seen our father protect our mother. The dynamics of Cece in the male group was important. She could offer her perspective as a female in a way that an all-male group could not understand. Similarly, she was able to get perspective from her brothers and protection whenever needed. In our group, we all valued her because she was smart and could hold her own in a group of strong men. She became another example of us creating a foundation for the type of people we had in our group, what we wanted to represent, and we were happy to provide a brotherhood to her. 'Good Fellas' is a complete unit, and we all represented the type of people we wanted around us; strong, smart, and role models for the community, and hopefully, our sons and daughters.

We all were aligned with our foundation of God, family, education, and goals, which made our crew so strong. We shared similar goals, and over time, we became one of the most popular and respected crews in the city. This notoriety was not based on being in the streets, but in being athletes, good students, respectful, involved in the community, and being goal getters. We were respected in every hood, respected by all of the adults in the city, and all of the youth looked up to us. We also threw some of the best parties ever to hit the city. From house parties, club parties, and even as we matured to community events, we were able to leave an impact on the city.

We stuck together and were always so strong because we held each other to a major standard of living. We all had keys to my parents' house since it was the safe haven; we slept head to toe with each other when needed, we ate together and practically did everything together. We never wanted to let each other down or want to be the one to ruin the reputation of our crew that we had all built together.

None of us would be who we are today without everyone in our crew. It is important to realize that every crew has its ups and downs, but there is not anything that should ever come between a crew. Our crew was built tough because nobody was ever a leader of our crew. We all lead in our own lives with the support of one another. If one of us had an accomplishment, we were all excited for them like it was our own. The group we have today has always been outlined by the key fundamental elements that I held growing up: Integrity, Honor, Respect, and Responsibility to be the best version of ourselves, earning every accolade through hard work and resilience.

When someone got into trouble, felt like life was too much, or needed someone, we were there at the drop of a dime for one another. That is just how we rolled, through creating a bond that money, cars, clothes, fame, or anything materialistic could never break. All of our parents and families became family, and the bond became stronger than just friends. So many praised us because of what we stood for and took pride in. A lot of our crew's characteristics never had to be spoken upon because real recognized real.

We had the best of both worlds growing up, meaning the book smarts and street smarts. The street smarts came from the respect of the streets. We had friends who were extremely close to us that strayed to the streets but always had the utmost respect for what we stood for. I am not talking about typical street involvement, but serious street guys who were willing to do anything to make sure we were straight, protected and never bothered by anybody because we gave hope to the city. We would walk in places, and people would show us so much love, which gave us the confidence that we really had something special.

There was rarely a time you would ever see just one of us, we got into many places for free and we really got the love that any street gang would get because we were "The Good Fellas." This is still the same foundation that has carried these friendships to this day. The consistency of our bond has maintained the bond between us all for decades. While many of our friends might have shifted in and out of our lives, our core beliefs and value system kept us together. It is essential that you build a team of like-minded people that you can grow and build with so that when you eventually become successful, you all can gain respect for doing what is right. These friends can ensure that you do not get into trouble and that you all can laugh, enjoy life together, and be around to reminisce about the memories.

Lastly, many authors speak about the core principles I discussed throughout this chapter. An example is a book called "The Pact." In the seventh grade, my mother bought me this book and it was one of the presents in my Easter basket. *The Pact* narrates the lives of Rameck Hunt, Sampson Davis, and George Jenkins, three young Black men that grew up in a community of violence, ignorance, and failure.

The book shows their first-hand experience of racism and the low expectations for their future. Eventually, the three made a promise that one day they would not only graduate from college but that they would graduate as doctors. They later received **scholarships** to **Seton Hall University**, although the process was difficult. Despite managing to overcome many obstacles to gain scholarships and attend college, they still ran into racism, mediocrity, and failure. At one point, the group talked about dropping out of college, but they were talked out of it by a guidance counselor.

They decided to face their obstacles and eventually graduate from Seton Hall. The three then studied to become doctors, with Hunt and Davis going to attend **medical school** while Jenkins decided to become a **dentist**. The book ends with all three of them passing and earning their medical degrees at their respective schools. "The Good Fellas" story is still to be written in its entirety, but trust and believe "The Pact" was impactful in helping us gel and become one. This was one of the best books I have ever read in my life, and the application of this book within our team holds true today. There is a pact amongst us to never give up on our dreams, and an understood agreement that none of us are allowing the other to give up, no matter the circumstance or perceived hurdles we face.

In life, you become a direct reflection of the five closest friends you have. As you reflect and relate to these stories, consider who your friends are and if you are beneficial to their lives like they may be for yours. If you have people in your direct circle of friends that are not on the same mental level as you, then you have some adjusting to do. As you reflect on those closest to you, take a moment to write down who your five closest friends are at the moment. Then, identify if you have common goals by writing 'yes' next to their name. If not, write 'no' next to their name. If you answer 'yes' by their name, keep them within your closest circle. If your answer is 'no,' identify if they are willing to make the adjustments necessary to clear their deficit. If this does not prove to be helpful, ditch them.

5 CLOSEST FRIENDS: YES, OR NO

1. _____
   _____

2. _____
   _____

3. _____
   _____

4. _____
   _____

5. _____
   _____

Chapter 2:

PREPARE TO OVERCOME ADVERSITY:

"A righteous man may have many troubles, but the LORD delivers him from them all." **Psalm 34:19**

Preparing to overcome adversity is essential as you live your life. There is a phrase that claims that God gives his toughest battles to his toughest soldiers. I believe this is true, which is why everyone in life has to face adversity, whether you like it or not. In this life, you can let the adversity make or break you. Adversity is something we face every day. Your confidence should always help you skyrocket through adversity. The time that you have a deadline to do your chores is a time of adversity. The time you failed a test because you did not study is adversity. The moment you tried out for a team but did not make it is adversity. The time you lose someone in your family is adversity. Losing your job is adversity. Adversity is not something you ever need to run from, but rather embrace. When you decide to embrace adversity and not complain about it, you grow as a person. It is important that you understand that everything you go through, you are supposed to grow through.

The way you react to adversity is your true test and ultimately exposes your true character. The way you react to adversity separates the real from the fake, the tough from the phony, and the lions from the gazelles.

The ones that survive adversity and do not let it break them are the ones that make it in life. Every bit of adversity you overcome should be treated as an accomplishment. Every bit of adversity that you overcome becomes a part of your history. As you grow, the small adversities that you overcome give you strength and help to prepare you for the greater adversities that you will face in the future. For me, I overcame a lot of adversity that many will never know. Females dissed me; I've failed tests, gotten cut from teams, lost games, lost money, friends, and family members, and everyone did not always believe in me. I have broken body parts and was not always the best at what I did. One thing I did generate was a competitive edge through overcoming adversity.

LIFE VS. SPORTS

I have always learned a lot from sports. I was a well-rounded athlete before basketball took over my life. I mean ball was life and still is. I grew up with a basketball court in my yard, and my brothers and The Good Fellas all torched me in basketball games. I was always the smallest, so they bullied the heck out of me. I loved playing so much that I would never quit, no matter how many times I lost. It got so bad that I would be outside on my own every chance I could get. I worked on my game so that I could challenge anybody who came out next, thinking I would win, and usually, I lost. With every game I lost, I became more confident. Although I'd lose many of those games, I managed to gain more points during each match. I knew that eventually, with more practice and greater determination to win, that I would eventually begin to win more than I'd continue to lose.

My friends and brothers made me work harder and making me tougher with every game. It got to the point where I started winning after years of playing, and then they could not tell me anything about playing ball anymore. I played on basketball travel teams with the St. Paul Warriors, the team my brother and his crew played on as well. I played for the Ben Franklin Academy Prep school team, the YMCA team, Boys and Girls Club, and in eighth grade- for the Harrisburg Cougars' middle school team after not getting picked for the freshman team. I knew then that it was my time to shine. After a great year with my coaches, Al Cloud and Jason Lester, I managed to learn how to be a real point guard. I knew I would be ready for my freshman year.

Al Cloud became a real big brother to me and not just a coach, but as someone who saw the potential in me and ensured I was prepared for success both on and off the court. I got so good that I became a freshman and jumped right into the junior varsity team. The team and I had a really good year while I was the freshman point guard, leading the team and rarely ever losing a game.

After that, I knew that it was time to take over being a Harrisburg Cougar point guard, following the team blueprint of Alphonso "Fonz" Burnett and Tamir "Puka" London, two of the greatest point guards I ever witnessed from Harrisburg.

I remember watching Fonz's team win the State Championship in 2002 and wanting to be just like him. He knew I was going to be the next great point guard, and he told me, "Lil Cuz, you're up next. Your team will only go as far as you take them." I was then ready for sophomore year and planned to take over playing point guard, only to hit the biggest roadblock in my life at that time. Up until then, I was always prepared, I was ready. I put in the work, and whatever the coaches needed me to do, I did. I was war-ready. I had more pride in being a Cougar than anyone possibly could at that time. Then adversity hit me with a jab, uppercut and right hook to stagger me and almost knock me out. My hopes of being the next great point guard diminished as I was benched all year long.

I was told that I was too good to play junior varsity again, but wasn't good enough to play varsity, a statement that crushed 95% of my soul. I acted out of character. I used foul language every day at practice, and I caused chaos every day at practice because I was not mentally prepared for the adversity that suddenly hit me. I did well in games that I was put into at the varsity level, even if it was for 7 seconds at the end of the game after already blowing a team out by 25 points as we used to do back in the day. Still, my mind was running crazy, and I wanted to quit. I wanted to hate my coaches and wanted the team to lose every game. I wanted to give up on basketball because I was not ready for the adversity that hit me.

Luckily, a man named Destry Mangus swooped in like Captain America in the summer of my eighth-grade year before entering high school and made me a part of his organization called Hard 2 Guard, a basketball program made up of older men. These men never had anything in life handed to them and worked for everything they had achieved. These men, Will Chase, Shawn Lewis, Al Cloud, Demone Maxwell, Larry Brown, Dave Archer, Jason Lester, Marc Lester, Micah Davenport, and Mike Geez, all took me under their wings and helped groom me as a young man. They had me playing in all the summer grown men leagues to help my maturation process. I really felt like their little brother. If someone fouled me too hard, they would check them. If I needed to work out, Shawn or Will accompanied me. Whatever I needed, they made sure I had because they saw the potential in me.

During that sophomore year, I called Shawn and Will every day, asking them why I was not getting treated fairly and why the coach did not like me. Their response was, "B, we've all been through this adversity that you are going through. You are not the first one and will not be the last. So, man up, embrace this adversity and let it make you, not break you." Hearing from those guys so often saved my basketball career. The season went on, I stuck it out, still having resentment and hatred in my blood towards my coaches. By the grace of God, and guidance from the elders, my parents and friends, I did not quit. I then decided to work so hard that there was no choice but to start me as a junior and senior for the Harrisburg Cougars and become one of the best point guards to ever suit up in a Harrisburg Cougar uniform. Those moments in time were an example of the adversity that I would face in life and put everything my father said would happen in my life during our Saturday morning talks into play. My father gave me the verbal experiences, while my coaches gave me the living circumstances that I needed to implement what my father had prepared me for all along. I learned how to win, how to lead, how to be verbal, how to give and take direction, how to listen more than talk, and how to comprehend and implement. I became the ultimate floor general, learning how to become relentless and fearless. This adversity sparked my flame and gave me a sense of who I could become if I challenged myself through troubling times. It taught me how to shine when the lights were faint, as well as when they were bright. Meaning, I had to learn to remain consistent in my abilities and discipline, whether I was in a moment of triumph or working through defeat. As a result, I became the ultimate student-athlete from Harrisburg, a city where so many student-athletes were counted out and not expected to ever make it out of the hood. The Hard 2 Guard family never let me quit and always supported me. I managed to use those moments of adversity as an example of resilience and perseverance.

That adversity prepared me for the next level of adversity that I would face. I was blessed enough to receive an academic scholarship to attend Susquehanna University, where my coach, Frank Marcinek, and I kicked it off from day one. He kept his promise that I would be able to compete as a freshman for the starting point guard role. I came, I saw, and I conquered as a result of the prior preparation and adversity I had to endure and overcome. College basketball and life lessons were extremely different. The game was faster, the players were better, and the life lessons I had to deal with were more so on my own or directly with my brother Erich. I won the starting point guard position as a freshman and never looked back.

I started every game four years in a row, clocked the most minutes ever played in history as the defensive player of the year three times, served as a two-year captain, and set records in assists and steals in a career, season and games. I learned that as you grow, God throws another test in your way, to test your faith, determination, drive, and will to make it in life, regardless of what you have to go through. It was a moment in time where I had to rely on my previous discipline and work ethic to make a name for myself at the collegiate level.

My father loved Susquehanna University and everything about it. I became extremely popular at school, but my dad was seriously famous there. He had his own VIP parking spot and seat at Erich's football games and for my basketball games. Before every game, I saw my father in the front row and would hug him at my home games or tap my chest two times at him at away games. My father and mother never missed either of our games, no matter what. My father was my Superman. He not only took care of his family and friends but despite his health issues, nothing could ever knock him off of his square, just like he taught us never to let anything knock us off ours. He overcame a variety of surgeries, his friends passing away, and situations you would not believe even if I explained them to you.

Life eventually caught up to him even after all of the adversity he overcame and the strength that was embedded in him. Unfortunately, he had to undergo heart surgery. Now, when someone hears that their father has to go in for heart surgery, the average person would fear what was going to happen next. My father did not have me bothered by any means because I knew how strong he was. I felt like nothing in life could knock him off his square. I remember my father and family preparing for the surgery like it was yesterday. It was crazy because he did not doubt that he would not make it through. I had so much confidence in him that I just knew he was going to make it through his surgery and that the doctors would do everything possible to bring him through since God was not done working on him. We got to the hospital, family and friends came to show him love and pray with him before the surgery. I just sat back and soaked everything in, not saying a word but looking at his charisma, charm, smile, laughter, and his ability to still entertain the room of visitors who came through to show him love. Wherever my father was, everyone knew it was going to be a great time, no matter the circumstances. If you did not know him, you would have assumed that he broke an arm or something and just had to get a cast the way he was in such good spirit. The looks on everyone's face was stunning because they all knew him as a man who would drop kick adversity in the face without a thought.

I saw tears from my brothers and those who were the last ones to leave his hospital room. I did not once saw a tear from my mother, who I was trying my hardest to stay strong for during his process. After everybody gave him their last words, it was just he and I left in the room. He grasped my hand tight; I told him, "I love you, man." Then I hugged him. He then said, "C'mon, B. Stay strong, baby boy, you know I will always be there for you, and that I will never miss any of your games." I told him I loved him, and he said the same back, then I told him, "I'll be here when you wake back up." His last words to me left me with so much confidence that he was going to hold on to his word and never leave me.

Then the surgery occurred. I left to go get some rest and pray, during that nap, I had a jet black dream where nothing happened. I was lying on a couch at my aunt's house when Westburn called me. I looked at my phone, answered it, and all Westburn could say was, "Come down to the hospital B." I yelled, "What happened, Wes?" He replied, "I will see you in a few minutes, bro. I love you." I rushed to the hospital, only to hear my father did not make it through. When we talk about heartbreak, being distraught, and crushed, that was me. I busted out in tears and disbelief in Garrett's arms, yelling, "Dad said he was going to make it!" Erich then came in, embracing the hug as Westburn came to add the final big brother touch to the hug and told all of his younger brothers, "It's time for us to step up to the plate as dad taught us." I could feel my mom looking at us from a distance before she came to close the family hug out. She looked as if she was proud of her and my father's body of work, raising us. She just made sure we realized our father put up the fight in life. She made sure we understood never to forget everything he taught us. Most importantly, what my father would always say, "In life you are born, you live and then you die, and you just have to always stay strong."

Now, I swore my father was the toughest in the world, but my mother never shed a tear in front of me ever. I know she grieved tremendously, but that woman never cried in front of me, which really showed how strong a woman she was. She made sure I knew she had to stay strong to ensure our family stayed strong and that I, as the youngest remembered what my father said: "You are the youngest, but you still have no excuse to be the weakest link."

My father's funeral was packed with family and friends from across the world. His funeral was so packed the pastor even stated, "I wish all of you would act like Big Wes passed every day so that this church can be packed every Sunday." That set off the perfect home going service that my father would have truly wanted. As my father's youngest son and the last person he ever spoke to, his passing became a turning point to catapult my life. I will elaborate on this in the next chapter. The great thing about adversity is that if you embrace it, if you grip it by the face and figure out ways to work through it, nothing will be able to knock you off of your square until God calls you home. You will eventually become so strong that you will be able to laugh at the thought of adversity. I faced so much more adversity that I learned to make overcoming it look easy.

I tell you this story because you will also face adversity, tons of it. Best believe that if it does not kill you, it will only make you strong. This adversity was a pivotal point in my life.

Understand that facing adversity is never easy, but it will always be worth it if you fight through it. As you go through life, it will be essential that you find ways to channel and redirect your frustration as well. For me, I used basketball, I used the weight room, I used writing, I used running, I used speaking, and most importantly, 'giving back' to my community all as ways to channel my frustration and overcome the adversity I was going through.

Basketball was an outlet because I could express every emotion through my effort. When I played the game of basketball, my passion would explode every second of every practice or game. I used the weight room as a tool because I knew I could throw weight around and not physically harm anyone, but as a way to enhance my strength to endure my journey. I used writing to channel my frustration because if I did not want to talk to anyone about what I was going through, I could always write to my father how I felt at the time. While writing to him, I would truly feel like he was having a full-blown conversation back with me. I used running as an outlet, as well. Running allowed me to build my endurance not only for basketball but for the lifelong journey I was on. I would get up and run the hills in Reservoir Park to condition my mind and my heart to be able to withstand any challenges. Lastly, I used speaking as an outlet because I eventually realized that speaking about my story would help someone else get through theirs.

One thing you have to realize in life is that what you are going through is not that bad. Someone in the world has it worse than you. So whatever cards you're dealt in life, you better play those cards with all your might, fight, and tenacity to make those cards work for you and not complain. Complaining about a situation does nothing but drag it out. After you are done complaining, you still have to find a solution. Just skip that complaining step; it is a waste of time. Learning to channel your frustration and using it as fuel to move forward in pushing through the adversity is what overcoming is all about.

With this in mind, create a list of five ways that you can channel your frustration after overcoming adversity. Write your five ways here, then continue to transfer your replies onto the same sheet as your spiritual, family goals, and other goal-setting answers from chapter one.

5 PERSONAL WAYS TO CHANNEL FRUSTRATION

1. _____

2. _____

3. _____

4. _____

5. _____

Chapter 3:

PREPARE TO DEMOLISH ALL COMPETITION

"For even the Son of man did not come to be served, but to serve, and to give his life as a ransom for many." **Mark 10:45**

Preparing to demolish all competition is a severe lesson. A lot of times, people are told that everybody is a competition. I was even told by someone in the community of Harrisburg, "as life goes on, if somebody is not with you, they are against you." When I heard that, it sunk in, and I started to believe that, then as I continued to grow and mature, I grew to hate that phrase. What the phrase "if somebody is not with you, they are against you" did was encourage me to shut out those who did not believe in me. I shut out those people who were not on my sports team, family members, lived in my community, teachers, or those who could not directly relate to who I was or where I was from. I grew to become boxed in, have limitations, and became programmed to a mediocre way of thinking. I was programmed to the mentality of only wanting perspectives from my lens.

GROWING UP FAST

I remember a time I was playing in the city's adult summer league with the Hard 2 Guard team. It was the summer after tenth grade's mind-boggling season, and a grown man told me, "You can't shoot, you will never be able to go to college, you will never be good enough." I flat out lost it on him. I even said some pretty foul things to that man, which I later never felt sorry for, until now as an adult. I did not believe that a grown man should have said what he said to me, especially at that time in my life. I was prepared to demolish him as my competition. One of the guys from the team overheard the man telling me this and came over really quickly and checked him, and even made him apologize to me. At that point in my life, I used him as my motivation, when in all actuality, his career was long gone, and he could not stand a chance against me. I then added his words to my memory bank and used them as fuel to my flame to spark up my junior year.

During my high school seasons, if someone was not on my team or went to my school, I rarely talked to him or her. One of my best friends,

Tramayne Hawthorne, went to a rival school, and he was extremely good at basketball. We grew up together, spent summers together, and traveled together, but when school started, we never talked until the basketball season was completely over. He was not at my house, nor was I at his, and we did not support each other because I was taught to become enemies at that time. I was prepared to demolish him as my competition. I became a role model strictly for my own city. I was highly respected for being the star basketball player and student; I visited elementary schools to read to the students, sign autographs, talk to teachers, and went to youth sports games to take pictures with them. I only allowed myself to become accessible to my own community and decided not to spread my love, wisdom, knowledge, and positive energy amongst any other surrounding areas. I became truly boxed in and closed off.

I had to learn that I could not try to demolish other people and that I had to diminish any negative characteristics I had, which became my true challenge. I had to demolish the laziness that often occurred when it came to self-accountability. I had to learn not to wait for someone to hold me accountable but rather hold myself accountable. I had to take pride in not having to be told to do something more than once, and I had to become more cautious of my language when playing sports and in other environments. When I realized that I did not have to compete with others but rather focus on my characteristics and attributes, I became an even better young man. I started to understand the importance of how the little things in life prepare you for the bigger things in life. I then began the process of demolishing all of my negative characteristics. At this point in my life, I really started to implement who my father was into who I was becoming. I started to take control of my actions, thoughts, and outcomes, which goes back to that addition problem of Positive Thoughts + Positive Action = Positive Outcomes. My smile got brighter, my love started to spread, my care for others increased, my swag began to peak, my relationship with God got stronger, my abilities in basketball got better, and my work ethic became stronger just like my father's.

I was beginning to make the shift from who I thought I wanted to be and who I needed to become to achieve better results. I took the lessons from my father and began to implement them into my everyday life.

I began to experience things in life that helped keep me in line with who I wanted to become. Once I got rid of the negative, I hit a turning point in my life. My father's passing was the hardest thing I had to cope with in my life by far. I mean, nothing in the world can compare to me losing my father or mother. In losing my father, I realized that nothing else could stop me from who I wanted to become. When my father passed away, I was so frustrated with life that I blamed anything besides my family for his loss. I faded off of friends. I was almost ready to forget all of what was instilled in me. I hit rock bottom when my father passed away. I was a sophomore in college with limited income, and I refused to ask my mother for help, as I was beginning to feel that there was no point in living. I was willing and ready even to start to sell drugs. I made a call to someone who was a mentor of mine but still affiliated in the streets. I explained to him my situation and told him, "Big homie, I am ready to cross over." In my mind, I was ready to cross over, and not cross over on the court, but cross over from the court to the streets.

By the grace of God, I grew up in a solid foundation, I took pride in that foundation, built my reputation and made my goals known to everyone who I knew had my best interest at heart. When I told him my thoughts, he laid me clean. He gave me one of the 'realist' talks I ever had with someone. He told me how I was the future and how I gave hope to the city. He reassured me that my father would not want me living that lifestyle, how the streets were not worth the risk, and that the streets would ruin my blessings. He told me I am more of a blessing by being in college and playing ball than any amount of contribution that I could make to the streets. He reminded me that my purpose was on the basketball court, and not in the streets. He even said, "B, you tripping if you thought you were going to call me, and I'd give you drugs. Your mom and dad would kill me if I did, and I better not ever hear that you have any, or you and I are going to have a problem." He made sure I realized that I knew I was born to use my life, courage, experiences in a positive light to others so that I could be a blessing to them. At that moment, he provided the perspective needed to reassess what it was that I was entertaining. He reminded me of my father's expectations and my promise to him to stand behind the family name by respecting and honoring the Major's name.

This man saved me from going to the streets. I could have called plenty of street guys, but God directed me to call this special person to help redirect my life to what His plan is for me. It is important that you seek positive guidance. If you are not placed around positive guidance, you have to be willing to go seek it. Many positive adults have a genuine love for youth who want help in reaching their full potential in life. If you seek your community leaders, the role models, athletes, politicians, and whoever you may look up to, you have a great chance of them becoming your mentor. As you become a protégé of someone you idolize, their network will become yours, which in your future can have a great impact on your net worth.

This example is evidence of why all of the goals you have written down already as so essential. God knows I am one of His strongest soldiers, and He realizes that if you are reading this then you are as well. This experience triggered me into demolishing the lingering negative thoughts or actions that I had within from when I was scared to stand up to the adversity I was facing. This was pretty much the first and last time I ever questioned God's work. I was so upset with God for taking my father away from me because I was selfish. I did not realize that my father applied God's mission for his life by instilling those lessons in me before he departed.

My father impacted so many lives. He was alive and present to raise his family. The only woman I ever saw my father with was my mother. My father was one hundred percent in all of our lives. My father shared every ounce of knowledge, wisdom, and guidance about life, girls, partying, money, school, life skills, and God that he had in him. Most importantly, he raised my brothers and me all into men before leaving us.

It is extremely important that you are placed around positive people who have a genuine love for your well-being, respect for your family, respect for you, and respect for your goals. My life from that conversation catapulted me over the biggest wall of adversity I had ever faced. Facing adversity has and always will be a process. The only way to gain the confidence to even stand up in the face of adversity is to not back down from it. I share my experience with you to inform you that yes, you will face losses in your life of family members, friends, or loved ones, but what you have to appreciate is the knowledge and wisdom they share while they are here.

At this point, take a minute to reflect on five or more negative characteristics or attributes that you have that you need to demolish. Write them below, then on your sheet from chapters one and two.

CHARACTERISTICS TO DEMOLISH

1. _____

2. _____

3. _____

4. _____

5. _____

As I continued to read, accept mentors, go to college, and learn from the mistakes of others, I began to realize that I had no diverse cultural perspective or understanding. Coming from an African American community, I had no clue about how to function around or relate to other races. I was boxed in and felt like other races became a competition to me. I then had the experience of being in college and realizing that as people, we all have similar goals and aspirations, so we do not have to compete to demolish someone else. I came to terms with the idea that the only competition I have is myself. I learned that there was no reason to try to demolish someone else as I tried to better myself. You will hit a wall in life and realize that you are your own biggest competition. You have to prepare to become better today than who you were yesterday.

Chapter 4:

PREPARE TO BECOME BETTER TODAY THAN YOU WERE YESTERDAY

"For I know the plans I have for you, declares the Lord, plans for welfare and not for evil, to give you a future and a hope."
Jeremiah 29:11

When you become your own biggest competition, you will prepare to become better today than you were yesterday. You will begin to fear the person you see when you wake up in the morning, go to the bathroom, and look in the mirror. You will begin to fear yourself as a person because you know that person has a potential breakthrough that can change the world today. You will fear that person because that person is capable of living their dreams, and you know he or she will stir up conversation throughout the world. That person will be you, and you have to be willing to look at yourself in the mirror and stare into your own eyes, telling yourself that you are never going to give up and must be willing to keep that promise to yourself. Becoming better today than you were yesterday is built strongly from your own goals that you have been creating while reading this book.

When my father passed away and following my mourning period, I had to get my life back on track. I was moving forward in such great faith that when he passed away, all of my faith went out of the window. After second-guessing God for days, I went back to my father's gravesite to have a conversation with him about life. I wanted to see what I should do next, how I should implement what he taught me without him, how to remain strong without him, and how to accomplish my own life goals without him. I remember just lying next to his grave and crying because he was gone, because he had to no longer suffer, crying because I had to man up, and crying because I realized I could not let him down. I then talked to him, thanking him for life, for being the leader of our family for so long, for teaching me so much, for leading by example, for putting life into perspective and giving me the confidence to move forward with my life in a way I would be able to make him proud and to give him something positive to talk about while he was in heaven.

As I sat by the grave, I had to ask him, "Pops, you told me you were going to be there for me. What happened?" All I could picture was his smile that could brighten up any cloudy day. During this conversation, I felt like he was replying to every thought I had, every question I had and gave me the guidance that he was always reliable for. By the time the conversation was over I felt extremely at ease, I felt like I could conquer the world, I felt like no adversity that I could ever face the rest of my life would stand a chance going up against me.

I had never felt so much pain and wanted to give up or quit at any point in my life until my father passed away. So many memories and life lessons went through my mind. It felt like he was passing the torch of his life over to me. My father passing on May 9, 2008, was bittersweet because it was the worst thing that happened in my life and also the best to happen in my life at the same time. The worse because I no longer had my father with me physically, and the best because my father was with me spiritually and became my guardian angel. Lastly, I remember praying the Lord's Prayer and answering all of the questions he would ask all of my friends. I started laughing so hard that my cheeks started to hurt like he and I would always do. I overcame this adversity in my life, so I truly believed that nothing else in my life would equate to this point. This gave me the wisdom that tomorrow is never promised, so you have to always master the day. I took a stand on May 15th, 2008, that I would make every day the best of my life to master every day of my life.

When you are preparing to become better today than you were yesterday, you have to really assess your history, your process, and, most importantly, your goals. Your history is essential because you have to know who you were before working on who you're becoming, and you need to know where you were versus where you are headed. History is something that always repeats itself, really like a cycle. For instance, if you were born into a family of doctors, you have a great chance of becoming a doctor. If you were brought up in a family of drug dealers, you have a great chance of becoming a drug dealer. If you are a part of a family who are goal-getters, you have a great chance of becoming a goal-getter. Lastly, if you were born into a family of athletes, you have a great chance of becoming an athlete. The cycle of the life you were born into cannot change, but you can change your outcome. While the likelihood of someone becoming what their family is runs high, every person has an opportunity to break their cycle if they wish to do it differently.

I was fortunate enough to be born into a life with a solid foundation, so it was only right to seize the moments and take full advantage of the life that my parents provided for me. I made sure I was an excellent child, brother, student, and athlete because I was grateful for the life I was given. I saw my mother going hard every day to make sure her family never wanted for anything. I saw my father working at all times of the day and night to make sure he could be the backbone of the family. I saw my mother, father, brothers, and friends living and chasing their goals. Being exposed to a God-fearing family, a family of goal-getters, a family of loyalty, family of honor and strength, it became a direct reflection of me. Just like I was blessed enough to be fathered into the type of family I was, I have friends who were not so fortunate, but did not let that stop them from living the life they dreamed of for themselves. Earlier, I spoke about those people who you have around you that help to make you who you are. Sometimes, we cannot all be fortunate enough to simply be brought into a good foundation, and that is when some of us will have to rely on having positive influences around us outside of the families we are given. While the family is important, we all understand that we do not all enter into blessed situations. In order to handle adversity and become greater, sometimes we have to understand our surroundings and hold onto whatever areas of our lives have positive people in it, rather than surrendering to bad circumstances.

I have a mentor who was born into a life cycle of the street life. He lived on the south side of Harrisburg, PA, which is arguably one of the toughest parts of the city to break that negative life cycle of being street affiliated.

Through hope, faith, education, guidance, and a dream, he was able to break from a vicious cycle that seemed destined for him. Watching the Harlem Globetrotters basketball team in animation in the 1970s when he was growing up introduced him to the game of basketball. Through a combination of hope, faith, education, and guidance, he became a part of such an iconic organization. Through his process, he put himself on the map in numerous television commercials from 2000-2004, free-styling with other basketball stars like Paul Pierce and Vince Carter. The mind-blowing basketball skills he has displayed in those commercials were part of what brought him to the Harlem Globetrotters' attention. After he overcame his adversity during his journey, he began to live his childhood dreams, and now will go down as a legendary Harlem Globetrotter.

With that being said, if he can come from a life where he was counted out by society and by statistics, you can as well. His faith allowed him to break the negative life cycle he was a part of because no matter who or what counts you out in life, God will never count you out. If you are not dreaming while sleeping or daydreaming while awake, you are not living. Dreams are what make life worth living. Dreams help you get from what you were born into to who you want to be, or even who God wants you to become. Everybody has the capabilities to change what they do not like about their life if they really put their mind to it and make wise decisions.

After you know your history, you have to believe in your process. You have to believe that every day is a chance to be successful. Understand that you cannot fall in love with success before falling in love with the process. We are not often exposed to a person's stories and trials as much as we are exposed to their success. You will see someone with the big car, homes, money, luxury, and all of the material things but never understand the process that it took to get there.

Being in love with the process means starting with the end in mind, but it also means being able to understand that the process is a necessity. The process is what gets you the ultimate success, so there has to be a focus and a commitment to complete the process in order to achieve the goal. This is something that was taught to me back when I was a younger man trying to finesse chores. As I mentioned earlier, I quickly had to understand that there was a process before getting what I wanted, and that process could not be missed or skipped.

You have to be fully committed and invest in your goals. Imagine if you fully invest yourself into whom you want to become, without excuses, and just throw yourself at your goals. I guarantee you will reach goals that you could not imagine. Being connected and committed to your process brings along blessings that come along with the commitment process. There are smaller lessons and blessings that you pick up along the way, and those pieces are needed to complete the bigger picture. Many people are casual with their goals but not fully committed. The only time you will reach your peaks in life is if you commit yourself. You cannot have one foot in your goals and one foot out. Your process must mean more than that to you. Along your process, you cannot only wish for your goals, but you have to work towards your goals relentlessly.

So many people in life are talented and blessed with gifts that make them extremely unique, but never fully commit to their process and eventually never reach their goals. See, greatness cost nothing but your work ethic, which is free. If you are not willing to go through the process in order to prosper, then you need to re-evaluate your goals. Everything in life is a process, so you have to decide what processes you want to endure. If you are not committed, you will not make it. If you have goals and commit to them, they will come to pass. God already kick-started your goals by allowing you to have them.

I had to commit myself to God, then committed myself to my family, education, and then ultimately, I could commit myself to my goals. This is how and why I am going to make it and why you can make it if you prepare yourself.

I was committed to God early on in life, which has resulted in blessings that I never have a clue where they came from or for what reason. I stayed committed to my family, which allows them to support my every decision and always want the best for me. Committing to your education is a never-ending process. I was always told you need to learn something new every day in order to evolve. I received my high school diploma, my bachelor's degree, all the way up to my master's degree because I was committed to my education. I followed the footsteps of my brothers, who were committed to their education as well. After four long high school years, when I walked across the stage to receive my high school diploma in 2006, I moonwalked like Michael Jackson across the stage out of joy. I felt like I was ready to conquer anything life could bring my way.

After four of the most trying years in my life in 2010, when I walked across the stage to receive my bachelor's degree, I once again moonwalked like Michael Jackson out of joy and in memory of my father. I was then challenged to go ahead to chase that next level of education, a master's degree in public administration.

SUDDEN TURNING POINTS

When I was in graduate school, I hit a turning point in my life that I knew would change the rest of my life. Certain people continued to come into my life and help steer me in the right direction in order to become better each day. I attended Penn State Harrisburg Campus, and one of the first people I met was my guidance counselor.

I met her, had a great conversation about who I was, and who I was becoming. Before I left, she looked me in my eyes, and she said, "You are going to be exactly who you say you are." I thought in my head, "You damn right I am. I have no choice." But out of my mouth, I said, "Thank you. That means a lot that you believe in me." She became a tremendous help in my graduate degree process.

I then received a two-year internship opportunity with one of my mentors, Chris Franklin's best friend, the athletic director of the college. At that point, I knew that God was continuing to work in my life because I was committed to Him and keeping Him as a priority in my life. I learned the ins and outs of being an athletic director, something I always wanted to do, and I received that experience to build my resume. While in graduate school, it hit me. I was up at 3:30 am one morning, thinking about my father and how I could continue to make him proud of who I was and who I was going to become.

That morning in my room, I prayed, I cried, I laughed, and God hit me dead in my face with my million-dollar idea that he already installed in me, but that I was now ready to receive. I showed God for years that I trusted his process for me, and then He gave me a dosage of His recognition in return. I was thinking about a business that would allow me to keep my father's legacy alive. I remember going through so much preparation to get to where I was and had taken such pride in my last name, and suddenly… there it was: Major Preparation.

I told myself, "I have been through some Major Preparation, which helped me become who I was, and who I was going to become in the future." From that point on, I knew that this tagline would be my business. I started right then and there, thinking about all the business information I learned back in my School of Business and Industry classes in high school, looked online at business plan templates, created my mission and vision, then BOOOOM!, there it was.

I yelled across the hall to my brother, Garrett, telling him to come to my room so I could talk to him. I explained my idea to him, and he said, "Yea, that is Major. You have to take that and run with it. Make it happen; I got your back." I was hyped! I felt like I hit the jackpot, and my big brother believed in the idea, so I knew it was on like popcorn.

The next morning, I went to talk to my dad at his gravesite to tell him the idea and could feel him smiling down on me, which was more confirmation that it was that million-dollar idea that God blessed me with. I knew that I could get better every day of my life for the rest of my life to make Major Preparation the best business and program in the world that emphasized helping others prepare mentally, physically, emotionally, and spiritually to accomplish their goals.

I then had to create a logo. Not just any logo, but a logo that would be able to make an impact on the world similar to Nike or Under Amor. My logo eventually came to me from my father, my guardian angel. The wings represent my father, who transitioned from my living hero to my guardian angel. The wings remind me that I have the power to soar over adversity, the power to fly and lead communities like eagles, and the power to go get what I work for in life. The shield represents my father's fraternity, which was their symbol as well. The shield reminds me that I have the protection to shield any negativity, to block all the haters, to hide behind my shield, and focus on my priorities and that I have the force to run through any adversity that may come my way without worry or fear. I then thought of a slogan that would be catchy and ring a bell every time someone heard it. My father always taught me that you never deserve anything you do not work for, but if you do work, you get results, so there it was: Major Work = Major Results.

I knew I was not building this brand to chase money but for the love of my father, for my mother, brothers, the world, and for the love of seeing others succeed. I realized that if I chase the goal that the money would follow.

I committed myself to live a Major Prep Lifestyle. Living a Major Prep Lifestyle is based upon living your life, unlike most people who do not want to or are scared to because they do not realize their full potential. Living a Major Prep Lifestyle is being willing to work harder than the normal individual. Living a Major Prep Lifestyle is being bold enough to live your life in the present with the end in mind. Living a Major Prep

Lifestyle is having the willingness to sacrifice short term gratification for long term success so you can live the rest of your life like most people want to but are not willing to put the work in for. Living a Major Prep Lifestyle is being willing to do right in a world of people who may do wrong. Living a Major Prep Lifestyle is having the self-confidence to understand that your life is meant to be a part of history. Lastly, living a Major Prep Lifestyle is being brave enough to overcome adversity and help others on your journey to success day after day to become better today than you were yesterday.

In order to become better day after day, you have to create an effective routine for yourself. Whoever you believe is successful at a career similar to you, you need to figure out what their routine has been to become successful so you can outline their footsteps and add your own twist. You do not have to recreate your world. You just have to find gaps in the routines of others and capitalize on their mistakes. For instance, I am a basketball trainer, and I believe I am the best in the world. The only problem is the world does not know I am the best in the world. I do not have the most clients yet, I do not make the most money yet, but I plan to because I work, I study other trainers, I read, and never stop learning. I started my training company, and I reached out to a world-known established trainer name Gannon Baker. He worked with Kobe Bryant, Vince Carter, Carmelo Anthony, LeBron James, Derrick Rose, Kevin Durant, and many more NBA stars. I realized that in today's world, it is easy to contact certain people that you can relate to or want to have a connection with through social media.

I then found him on Twitter, sent him a message about training, and he replied right back to me, inviting me to come to his basketball trainer convention in Florida. All I had to do was buy my flight, and he said he would pay for the rest of the trip. I scrambled up all the money I needed from my family and bought the ticket three days later. I made it to the convention and came to find out there were sixty other trainers there. I felt so prepared and so confident that I walked into the room knowing I was the best in the world at our craft, mainly because I won each day of my life, and I was committed to my life for so long to be better than I was day after day. My charisma, my charm, and my persona stood out like a barefoot.

I sat in the front of the room, spoke up every chance I could, and made sure the room was unable to forget my name. I built relationships and asked questions of the other trainers who were there, and came to find out that I was the most prepared for the convention. Gannon Baker, a world-wide trainer whom I had never met me until that day, could look at how I engaged the room and the way I created separation from everyone else and see that I was going to be somebody. Today, Gannon and I are still friends, and he has become a mentor to me as I grow my business.

While at this event, we learned a ton from Gannon Baker about training and building your business, but the highlight of the convention was being able to hear NBA Champion Assistant Coach Kevin Eastman from the Boston Celtics who explained to the crowd the importance of one's routine. Hearing an NBA Champion coach speak on his routine and preparation was confirmation that the path I was on was going to make me **#BeMAJOR**. Kevin Eastman ended the conversation explaining to us all how Ray Allen's routine before every game was the best and most effective he ever witnessed. Ray Allen goes down as one of the best shooters in NBA history. Not because he was just skilled but because of his strict, consistent routine that he committed to daily. Before every game, Ray Allen would be at the gym three hours before the game to make shots on both ends of the court, the same shots each pre-game, with the exact same start time.

I left that meeting not star-struck or extremely impressed because I worked just as hard myself my whole life. I had my routine and goals in line already, and I was committed as well. Again, it was just confirmation that what my parents, brothers, and mentors all told me prior to attending this convention was being confirmed. You will learn that the same positive messages that people you know tell you will be the same positive message that those who you do not know personally will tell you. Yes, a message coming from a celebrity or star may seem unique, but the ones closest to you will have more of a sense of care and love for you than one who does not know you. A person closest to you also knows you personally and can speak more clearly to your purpose. Do not minimize the people around you and their words of encouragement.

I did not understand that positive messages all sound the same, but sometimes it will not click until someone you look up to says the same thing. I remember when I decided that basketball was what I wanted to do. My father told me to make sure I do my sit ups, pushups, toe touches, and squats every day. I did not think my father knew what he was talking about. Then after a workout with a man named Will Chase, I got in my father's car, and before Will said goodbye he told me, "B, make sure you do your sit ups, pushups, toe touches and squats." Initially, I felt like my father told him to say it, but he never did. So guess what, since Will was a guru of basketball and told me to do the exercises, I did them nonstop every day on. If I had listened to my father years prior telling me that same thing, I would have been even stronger than I was. It was a great turning point and lesson that I will never forget, to sometimes just shut up and listen the first time. Today, as a business owner, I created a five-step routine that I implement every day. Every Sunday, I create a 'To Do' list for every day of the week, which helps kick off my daily routine. By listening to the advice given by those around me, I am able to create a lifestyle that gets me positive results. The following is the well-known Major Preparation Routine

THE BRYAN MAJORS 'MAJOR PREPARATION' ROUTINE

Step One: Wake up and Pray
Step Two: Read daily Bible verse
Step Three: Work out to help eliminate any daily frustrations.
Step Four: Review & Execute checklist
Step Five: Morning Affirmations/Pray

Most importantly, I do something every day to get one step closer to my ultimate goals. I know that success does not come overnight but comes over time, and each day is time passing. If you win each day, your ultimate goal will feel easier than it looks in being accomplished.

You have to take your time to reflect daily and understand that greatness takes time. Life is a marathon, not a sprint. What you physically do daily will determine your day, week, month, year, and future. You have to find out who has been successful and replicate their routine or create your own that you know will work for you. Time is the only thing in life that matters that you cannot get back, so your routine must be one that will hold you accountable, and help prepare you to become better today than you were yesterday.

Your routine is so essential because as you do something repeatedly, it becomes second nature to your lifestyle. Realize that your routine can become rich if you implement it the right way. Now it is time to dig deep, stop excuses, identify the adjustments, and create your own daily routine. This routine will force you to commit and give your all every day in order to win every day you are blessed to live. Create your own five-step daily routine here and transfer this information to your other goals sheet.

YOUR ROUTINE

Step One:

_____

_____

Step Two:

_____

_____

Step Three:

_____

_____

Step Four:

_____

_____

Step Five:

_____

_____

Having a routine will help you to become blessed with opportunities that will catapult your life continuously. For me, my routine assisted me with me the confidence to know that I can reach whatever goals I work for because each daily routine leads to small results daily. I have no doubt in my mind that my ultimate goals will be accomplished, and that your goals can be accomplished as well. "Think It, Speak It, Claim It, Work for It, and Go Get It" is the motto that I tell myself when it comes to my ultimate goals. There is extreme dominance in your thoughts, words, claims, work, and what you can receive.

I had to face the fear of not being able to reach my goals, not being able to keep my father proud, not being able to carry the weight of success I worked for, so I snapped into what I call 'Major Prep Mode.'

'Major Prep Mode' is a mode that I turn on every morning that I wake up to let myself know it's time to win no matter what. It reminds me that I have goals to meet, that nothing can stop me but me, and that if God woke me up, then He blessed me with another twenty-four hours to get it done. So I challenge you to snap into 'Major Prep Mode' each and every morning to expose those special capabilities that you have in you to get to your ultimate goals. Having an ultimate goal is different from daily goals. They are goals that will force you to stretch yourself, goals that will keep you up wild hours of the night, and goals that will never allow you to get complacent or satisfied.

Having ultimate goals has to become visual before you can ultimately go get them. At some point in elementary school, you may have had to create a vision board for your life. If you never did, then you should now. A vision board is created by cutting out pictures of all the things you value, work for, commit to, and prepare for daily from magazines, newspapers, internet, etc. You can find powerful words, powerful visions that stick out to you and even have things that show what you're thankful for now to help maintain a current level of appreciation. My vision board is of my dream to own sports complexes across the world, having the best and most impactful brand in the world, a huge house for my family and friends, cars, training youth, high school, college, and professional basketball players, and worldwide groups of youth who are Major Prep Cycle Breakers to carry on the legacy forever.

By showing myself my dreams, it gives me the drive to go out and make sure I make the vision a reality. Take thirty-one seconds to close your eyes and think about your ultimate goals. Do not write them down just yet, but let them ponder in your thoughts. Then before you read the next sentence, take another thirty-one seconds to ask yourself if you are willing to commit to your routine to prepare to make your goals become reality. Prepare to overcome adversity. Prepare to demolish competition and prepare to become better today than you were yesterday.

Chapter 5:

PREPARE WITH INTEGRITY, CONFIDENCE & HUMILITY

*"Humble yourselves, therefore, under God's mighty hand, that he may lift you up in due time." **1 Peter 5:6***

If you are going to be bold enough to go after your goals, then be bold enough to have integrity, confidence, and humility. Having integrity in life is essential because it tests your true character as a person. If you are in a room with $100.00 that you know is not yours, but know if you take it, there is no way you can get caught, this will test your character. If you take the money, the person whose money it was may never catch you, but God, the ultimate person you have to answer to, will see you. So having integrity is doing the right thing even when you think no one is watching. Having integrity will keep you out of your own way of success. Not having integrity will block your own blessings. Integrity is something that allows me to carry on my father's legacy and find value in how we carry our last name. We move with integrity, whenever any of the Majors are mentioned, people associate us with honesty, respect, and integrity. Had we made different choices and acted dishonestly or disrespectfully, our names would be associated with negative things. Integrity is how you move and behave. This is critical to not only how God rewards you, but in how the world rewards or assists you with the resources needed to achieve your dream.

TESTING YOUR LIMITS

When I was about ten or eleven years old, I started to test my own limits. When my mom would go to the grocery stores, I would always go with her so I could use that charm and charisma that my father taught me on her to convince her to buy me stuff, since my brothers were not around to see her spoil me. This lasted until she caught on to my game. She would always tell me I could get what I wanted as long as I did not tell my brothers. My mom got to the point where she would just tell me to get my coat and come on. I never questioned her about where we were going. I was just excited to be hanging out with my mom. Eventually, I slipped up and threw the situation in the face of my twin brother Erich after one of our fights by saying, "That's why mom loves me more than you because she always takes me to the store, buys me what I want and keeps you here at home because she loves me more."

After that, it was all bad. I should have never said that to my brother, and my mom continued to make me go to the store with her but now told me no when I asked for those extra things.

My next thought process was to get my own money, but I had no job and chore money was once a month. I then started to realize that my mother always kept cash in her pocketbook, so late at night, I would go take one or two dollars and stash them in my room. I did it so long and never got caught until the time I took a ten-dollar bill instead of a dollar bill out of her purse. My mom and I were at the store. She had all her groceries and paid the cashier. I then grabbed something off of the isle rack, went to buy it and pulled out a ten-dollar bill. My mom looked at me like I was a crazy man, gave me the look of death, snatched the stuff out of my hand, took the money, and whooped my butt from the store to the car. A dollar was never noticeable, but that ten dollars almost made me lose my life. After that incident, my dad found out and whooped my butt too. This was definitely a lesson in integrity I will never forget. I had no reason stealing from my mother, but thought I could because I thought she was never going to catch me. From that point on, I attacked life with integrity day after day.

I realized that the incident could have ruined my mother's trust in me, and my father would be disappointed. Integrity challenges who we are, and it ends in how people view us for years to come. A poor lapse in judgment can affect people's impression of you. Integrity ensures who they see is someone worth respecting. I learned that there is always somebody watching, or that when you are doing wrong, you will always eventually get caught. I realized that having integrity will take me a lot further than I could ever imagine and save the skin on my behind. I began to act each day like my mother was watching my every move. I knew by having that mentality that my actions would line up with her expectations for me as her youngest son.

PREPARING WITH INTEGRITY

By living with integrity as an intricate part of my maturation process, I began to gain confidence in myself. Once that turning point hit me, my confidence skyrocketed out of this world. I just had the mindset that if I do things the right way all my life, then I will eventually get blessed with the capability and strength to endure my major preparation process. I knew it would be possible to achieve my goals. I never suffered from goal blindness. Along with gaining confidence and having integrity, I realized that the odds against me achieving my goals did not matter. I accepted that I had whatever I needed already inside of me in order to become legendary in the world. I walked with my head held high every day, I spoke with pride and I was not afraid to live my dream. I refused to die an unlived life. The ideas that I had, I always acted on because I had the confidence to go get them. I never wanted to die with great ideas stuck inside of me, with my leadership abilities stuck inside of me, with fear holding me back, and I declared to live my goals. There was nothing that I thought I could not achieve.

PREPARING WITH CONFIDENCE

Preparing with confidence helps you leave a bold statement with your life. Having confidence helped me increase my goals and challenge myself daily. I had to raise the bar for my daily expectations, never questioning how I would accomplish my goals, but just being mindful that they needed to get done. I talked to myself in the mirror daily to boost myself up about how hard living my goals will be but how worth it things would be ten years down the road. I committed myself to my goals and worked relentlessly on accomplishing them. Having confidence was essential for me on the basketball court and in real life. On the court, I believed I was the best point guard on any given court at any given time.

I played with so much confidence that I gained respect from many other players. My confidence on the court was so strong that coaches of opposing teams would speak to me after the games about how confident a player I was. The confidence I had in myself most importantly forced my teammates to raise their level of confidence in themselves. I just wanted to make every player, coach, or fan that witnessed me play basketball remember my name the rest of their life. I would hear stories about other players before me, and I wanted people to speak about me ten years later as they did about other basketball players like Michael Jordan or Allen Iverson.

The time I played high school basketball was a turning point in my career. My high school basketball program had a history and legacy for never losing home games, and I had to do all in my power to maintain the legacy. Picture this: Fourth quarter, with six seconds on the clock. We were down three points and had to go the full length of the court to score and send the game into overtime. Prior to the play, my coach created a play to have the ball inbound to me, so that I could speed past everyone and get the ball to our three-point shooter (which I thought was a great idea). We broke the huddle, and I had all of the confidence in the world that we were going to convert the last play of the game to go into overtime. It was on!

The ball got into my hands. I broke the defense and got the ball to the shooter, so I figured my job was done, thinking he had the ball and was going to nail the shot. What really happened was he did not have the confidence to take the shot because of all of the pressure, and he passed the ball right back to me. Without a second thought, I shot that ball with all the confidence in the world and nailed the shot from three! The crowd went crazy, coaches went crazy, and I went just as crazy. I ran to the middle of the court, started pounding my chest, screaming, "This is my house."

Before that point of the game, I did not score or have a shot attempt. The shot I took was the one that mattered the most. We went into overtime, and in the huddle, I just smiled at my coaches and teammates, then told them, "No way am I going to let us lose, I work too hard for us to lose on my watch." I had the confidence to take the shot because of my prior preparation. We won the game, and it felt amazing knowing that my preparation allowed me to prosper.

When I first joined the Susquehanna University Men's Basketball team, I was a freshman who came with confidence that I was going to take the current point guard spot and never give the spot back up until I graduated. I did just that, outworking every other point guard on the team and all those who came into the program year after year. That confidence

I played with helped groom me into becoming arguably one of the best point guards to play for Harrisburg High School and Susquehanna University.

The confidence I used on the court transitioned off of the court. No matter which classroom I walked in, I felt like I was the smartest in the room because I studied hard. Any time I had to speak at an engagement, I knew I would do great because I went over the speech one hundred times beforehand. When I went into interviews, I was confident because I researched all aspects of the job description. Confidence comes from prior preparation. It was self-confidence that people could see, and they respected it.

As you have integrity, confidence builds. As your confidence builds, you begin to have success. When success comes, you have to have humility in order to keep success coming and reach new levels of living. Having humility goes an extremely long way. Having humility means to always remain approachable, teachable, and coachable. Having humility is never thinking you are too good for others, no matter their circumstances.

When you have humility, it shows in your character and will help you be blessed on your journey to success. Confidence should always be coupled with humility.

Being approachable is essential because you never know what kind of impact you may have on someone who may be reaching out to you. Being teachable and coachable are critical attributes of your character, or else you will eventually block your own blessings. Humility is a characteristic that can build or break your name and reputation. You can be that person who is arrogant, disrespectful, not teachable, prideful, and egotistic and never reach your full potential. You can also choose to be humble enough to remain caring, respectful, approachable, and teachable and receive an overflow of blessings throughout your journey. There is no continued success without a humble spirit. Confidence is only good so long as it can encourage others to become their best. It should never be a tool to tear others down, but a tool to encourage those around you, including yourself.

PREPARING WITH HUMILITY

Preparing with integrity, confidence, and humility all have a direct correlation with one another. The morning I received my master's degree, I had so much to be thankful for and even more to look forward to. My graduation day was double-booked with a 'Build Your Business Boot Camp' in which I was a contestant. The BYBBC is an event in which, year after year, entrepreneurs are able to come and pitch their business proposal to a panel of judges and audience. The incentive was a cash prize for the top three contestants. There were seven contestants during this camp, prior to the day we had to pick out a number from a hat to decide which order we would go. Of course, I picked number one, which meant that I had to present at the same exact time of the start of my graduation.

There was no way I wasn't going to my graduation, so I had to share my dilemma with the BYBBC and ask to go last in order to make time to get back from my graduation and present my business plan. Luckily, the coordinator of the BYBBC was already one of my mentors, and he allowed me to switch to go last and said I would be able to present as long as I got there before the sixth person finished their presentation. The whole time I was at my graduation, I was enjoying the moment but could not stop looking at my watch, checking the time, or stop texting my mentor to make sure I had time. My name was finally called to cross the stage. I, of course, moonwalked across that stage as I did in high school and undergraduate school one more time, which made everyone in the stadium laugh. When I got back to my seat my mentor had sent me a text letting me know I had forty-five minutes to get there, the ceremony was still not over, the drive was twenty-six minutes away, and I still had to take pictures with my family and friends after the ceremony. I told myself to just have faith that I would get there in time.

The graduation ceremony was finally over, the pictures were taken, and I ran to my car. I hit that highway, was down to thirty minutes before I had to be there. By the grace of God, I did not hit any traffic, and I had my foot on the gas as I cruised to the presentation location, while feeling like I was the king of the world because I received my master's degree and saw that special smile that my mom gets when she is extremely proud. I got there, texted my mentor, and he told me I was lucky because I only had three minutes remaining. I walked in the location, having to pass all of the other contenders, and from the look in my eyes, my confident walk with my head high and chest out, they just knew I was about to murder that presentation. They all walked in before me to hear my presentation,

I told my mentor I was ready and gave him my materials to set up. He introduced me with so much pride and joy in his voice. He could not stop smiling and looking over at me as he was giving my introduction.

I walked in that room with so much confidence that even the panel judges just smiled and got ready to hear me speak. I was so confident. I walked into that room with the cap and gown on from my graduation and gave the best speech to that date about my business. I spoke with so much passion, pride, confidence, humility, and joy that I won first place and a cash prize. I was the youngest entrepreneur there, coming in high off of another accomplishment; I knew those guys did not stand a chance once it was my turn. I answered every question the judges asked, looking them dead in their eyes so they could feel my words and see the passion in my eyes.

When I won, every judge and the entire audience gave me a standing ovation for receiving my master's degree, winning the event, and having so much integrity, confidence, and humility while doing so. I prepared to be able to surpass basic expectations in moments like these. I grew to have so much confidence that I expected to win this event. When your confidence grows, your expectations for your performances have to rise as well. Winning that BYBBC was a turning point in my life, it showed me that Major Work = Major Results.

Preparing with integrity, confidence, and humility assist in enhancing your maturation process. In life, many people try to embrace immaturity so long that they block their own blessings. You may even know friends or family members who never wanted to mature. What people fail to realize is that the sooner you do things the right way, the more longevity you tend to have. For instance, every community has people who, at the age of twelve, were immature, at age twenty-four were still immature, and then finally, at age forty-eight, decided to become mature, expecting others to trust their words or actions. At that point, that person looks back and regrets his or her actions because they never displayed integrity, confidence, or humility before. See in life, if you operate with integrity, confidence & humility, people will take you seriously and help you gain that advantage to accomplish your own goals.

Take a moment to look back on your own actions when you had to implement integrity, confidence, and humility. Write three times when you had to encounter your own sense of integrity, confidence, and humility. Write your examples here and then on your paper, so you can stay consistent on addressing who you want to be, and how you want to get to that level.

WHEN I HAD TO IMPLEMENT HAVING INTEGRITY

1. _____

2. _____

3. _____

4. _____

5. _____

WHEN I HAD TO IMPLEMENT HAVING CONFIDENCE

1. _____

2. _____

3. _____

4. _____

5. _____

WHEN I HAD TO IMPLEMENT HAVING HUMILITY

1. _____

2. _____

3. _____

4. _____

5. _____

Chapter 6:

PREPARE YOURSELF TO NEVER GIVE UP OR GIVE IN

"But as for you, be strong and do not give up, for your work will be rewarded." **2 Chronicles 15:7**

Prepare yourself to never give up or give in. The Major Prep Lifestyle is already in your DNA. You already have those unbreakable/unshakable abilities that cannot ever be stripped from you. You may ask how one maintains this uncommon faith. Well, that is simple. You must work daily! Some people work sometimes. Training For Triumph requires you to work all the time every day! You see, if you work, you will have success, which breeds confidence. If you do not have success right now, you have to keep working and do not give up. Living a Major Prep Lifestyle is authentically different. You have the capability to focus on being the best at your craft. Yes, going after your goals is going to take you living an uncommon life and not wanting to be average. Just ask yourself, do you want to make it in life and be successful? If so, then you cannot follow the norm. You cannot try to be like everyone else. You have to solely focus on achieving your goals or "die trying."

In my eyes, living a Major Prep Lifestyle is normal, I am extremely blessed, and you are too. Understand that a part of being blessed is not having self-doubt, insecurity, or even a fear of failing. You see, two of the most common human characteristics are fear and laziness. However, you do not have to succumb to either. You have the capability to observe problems and finds solutions. You have the option to complain or compete. If you complain, it may ease your thought process momentarily, but those tasks in life have to be completed regardless of the complaint in order for you to make progress. To complain is to waste your own time and the time of others. Every day in life, you have the capability to add 'tools' to your 'toolbox' – that is add value to your life. These 'tools' are pieces that add value to your life.

By complaining, you remove the ability to keep building, and building is the only way to move towards progress. Complaining stifles growth and decreases your sense of confidence, simple as that.

It is possible for you to live your dream if you take personal responsibility to make it happen. You have to tell yourself that you are going to make it no matter the circumstances. As you are bold enough to live your goals, you have to be willing to take your leap of faith, stand up to the non-believers, stay locked in, and live your goals. You need to learn to activate your faith and not your fears.

After I earned my master's degree, I was blessed with the opportunity to move forward with my goals. I reached out to a local basketball trainer who had his own basketball training facility about wanting to work with him to help expand his business along with my own. We kicked it off right away. I was young, energetic, knowledgeable, and already established in the area, so I helped bring business in right away. We established a percentage split on profit, which was reasonable, so he made money off of me even when he was not in the building. I had to prove myself to him that I was willing to work with him. As I thought I was being beneficial to the gym, I think he thought I was being too influential with the clients. My training style, charisma, and work ethic started to become so impactful that clients started to think the facility belonged to me and only wanted me to teach the lessons. That did not sit well with him since he was the actual owner and operator of the facility.

When I taught classes at the same time he would, his clients would look down at what I had clients doing and how I had them advancing so fast that they wanted to join my program and leave his. There was even a time one of his best clients wanted to work with me instead of him, and he told the parents not to pay me, but pay him, and he would give me my split. That was not how our agreement was set up. He was not a happy camper about his clients wanting to work with me instead of him. I built relationships with new clients, parents, and a demographic that I never tapped into before. I could sense that my presence was not wanted much longer because of the conflict of interest.

Consequently, the friction grew. Even the clients could sense the tension between the two of us. The business was growing for me, and I was in a rhythm. I gained new clients and was building my brand while allowing him to make money off of me. I eventually ended up letting him know that I would no longer be training at his facility. Although I was unsure what would come next for me, I did not give up or give in. Most importantly, I did not fear the unknown. I considered that situation a chapter in my life that I would have to close and open a new chapter. The important lessons in those situations is to always take the benefits of what the experience has brought you, and leave the criticism with the experience. No sooner did I leave that facility than I was blessed with a greater opportunity.

One of my best friend's father was the Program Director of the Harrisburg Boys & Girls Club of America. He was looking for a new Unit Director for one of his facilities in arguably the roughest neighborhood in the city of Harrisburg. I had a relationship with him my entire life. He believed in the Major Preparation mission and in my capability to relate with youth. He believed in my connection within the Harrisburg communities and that I was the one who could help bring a bright light to a dark situation. I had a meeting with him and the Executive Director of the Boys & Girls Club of Harrisburg, and right then and there, they offered me the job. As soon as I was offered the position, the Program Director stated, "I do not expect you to be here for the rest of your life, but I want this position to catapult you to greater opportunities." I did not understand what he meant at the time; I was just happy that I had a job with benefits and a consistent two-week paycheck.

At age twenty-three I took on the responsibility of becoming a Unit Director in the south side of Harrisburg, at a club that was once led by a legendary man, Sherman Cunningham (Rest In Peace), whose footsteps I had to follow in order to revamp the vision of the Boys & Girls Club.

I accepted this position because I felt that it was God directing me to gain this experience and impact the lives of many who needed to visually see someone bold enough to chase their goals. I was prepared for the moment because of the way I lived my life.

When I started as Unit Director, I was like a tamed pit bull waiting to be let off the leash. Since I was not let off the leash, rather than be patient, I broke the leash and became the young wild pit bull who wanted to get things done right away. At this location, there was a time when hundreds of youth attended the club, but by the time I became Director, there were less than twenty children from a neighborhood of over thousands within walking distance of the club. The very first summer as the community realized I was the new Director, the number of youth who attended the club skyrocketed. Over one hundred youth were there on a daily basis under my direction, discipline, and influence.

Personally, knowing that so many others believed in me was a great feeling. Mothers and fathers of the youth constantly came and thanked me for the work I have done with their children in the community daily. Seeing the growth of the children I worked with was amazing. The relationships I built with them have become unbreakable. The youth in the area loved who I was, loved how I helped them prepare for their goals, loved the discipline and standards I held them to and loved the genuine care I had for their well-being. As Unit Director, I implemented the Major Preparation mission and the 11 Ways to Prepare Method in creating a new energy in that community. I turned the Boys and Girls Club of Harrisburg into the Major Preparation Cycle Breaker Club because the Major Prep way was the only I knew how to impact lives. The youth were there daily, wearing Major Prep clothes, had Major Prep book bags, and even yelled out "Major Work= Major Results" every time it was time to put in some work. The other Unit Directors were impressed with my work, and they felt like I was doing a fantastic job. They witnessed the improvement of the club, and they loved the new and revamped reputation of the legendary Boy & Girls Club in Southside Harrisburg, PA.

One particular Unit Director, David Smith, at the time, believed in the Major Preparation Lifestyle so much that he really triggered thoughts that I did not want to believe. He always reminded me to never settle for less than my worth and reminded me to never settle into circumstances that did not have direct positive relations to my ultimate goals for Major Preparation.

I started to experience certain situations that he would explain to me. Time after time, he would explain how things should be handled from the administrative level. Everything he was telling me was on point. Once again, I started to feel like I had the support of those who received immediate gratification from my presence, but not the ultimate support that I needed. My bold, engaged, confident, and knowledgeable charisma spoke volumes in a Major Prep way vs. Boys & Girls way. After a year of revamping and impacting lives, David told me, "B, you have to go, there is more for you, and you have a gift the world needs to know about. Home will always be here." By the grace of God and David, I was forced to take my leap of faith.

David enlightened my perspective about being a Unit Director and gave me the push I needed to take my leap of faith and begin my journey solely focusing on building up Major Preparation the way I wanted to without having to be under the direction of anyone. I had to stop coming up with excuses for why I was scared to take my leap of faith and just jump. Taking that leap of faith is not easy, but it's well worth the jump when you decide to. I was ready for the jump and just needed someone to push me off of the ledge.

LEAP OF FAITH

Before I took my leap, a friend sent me a YouTube video of Steve Harvey speaking on the fact that everything happens in your life to force you to take your leap of faith and become major.

As I took my leap of faith, I thought of how baby eagles are born in a nest. The parents may feed the eagle and show the eagle how to fly and survive, but then eventually, the eagle is forced to learn to fly and survive on its own. At first, the eagle is usually scared to leave the nest, believing that his parents will come back to save it, not knowing that its parents are long gone. The only option he has to survive is to take its leap of faith and leave the nest. By that time, the parents already know that the eagle has the capability to fly, and all it has to do is jump, sore into greatness and experience its amazing life as an eagle.

I then knew if an eagle could take its leap of faith and fly, then I definitely could take my leap of faith and soar throughout the sky as long as I never give up. As hard as it was to take my leap of faith and become an entrepreneur, I had to put my all into what I believed in. This became another turning point in my life. I told myself that I would never work full time for another company again as long as I live. I was open to partnering and being contracted, but never a full-time employee for another organization or company. At times, the adversity is just the motivator that you need to establish enough confidence and courage in your own brand. Had I not experienced those events, I might have still believed my purpose was best served under someone else. I found, in all of my power, that containing myself within other organizations was not only stifling my desire to be an independent brand, but it did not allow my ideas and freedom to be used in the best way possible. If I was to be happy and not in a state of complacency, I had to jump!

So, there I was, officially unsure of where I was headed, and only knowing I was never going to give up on chasing my goals for Major Preparation. I was eventually blessed with a meeting at the largest sports complex in the world. This facility is a dream complex for all athletes and sports. I met with the Sports Performance Director and had a great meeting. He then pointed me in the direction of the Basketball Director.

The Basketball Director and I had a great meeting the same day, and he left me with the impression that I would be the perfect person to be his assistant. This place was so fascinating that it had me blind to my original pact of not working full time for another company. I went through with the interview process and just knew that this opportunity would be the right one for me.

I became one of the final two contestants, which was a blessing. I did not know who the other contestant was, nor did I care. I just believed in myself and believed that this was my calling. I had my final interview and did a great job. I was not hired as the Assistant Basketball Director but was asked to be the basketball trainer of the facility. Little did I know it was a blessing in disguise that I was not hired for the position. God made it clear to me that I did not need to work for another company, even when I thought I would. Not getting offered the position was not a failure, but rather a 're-direct' from God to reposition my confidence back into myself rather than another organization. It was as if He sensed my hesitation and granted me another chance to clear my mind of self-doubt.

As the basketball trainer, the profit agreement was a 50/50 split. The company was not willing to pay for my travel, benefits, or pay me out of pocket themselves. I accepted the split for a year to show the company that I mastered my craft and proved that I could make them money along with growing my business. My clientele grew rapidly, so fast that I had to turn people away because my schedule was jammed-packed. I began to train professional basketball players and a great deal of the top-notch high school and college players in Central PA. Within a year's span, I generated $40,000.00 but had to give up $20,000.00. There was no way that after a year, I was going to allow myself to violate my brand. I was doing the entire training and a majority of marketing; all I needed them for was the space and lights. Once again, I started to feel boxed in and unappreciated.

When it was time to renew my contract, I had now asked for a 60/40 split to earn my worth without them having to pay me. They did not want to agree with the new deal. The company did not value or appreciate my worth. This wall of adversity felt so high that it seemed as if it would take forever to overcome. What I did not do was give up or give in to adversity. I welcomed it as a necessary challenge.

I had to go back to the drawing board and readjust. I informed all of my clients that I would no longer be training at that facility, and they were highly upset. In life, when the adversity wall goes up, you have to find a way to climb over, go under, around, or bust through that wall by all means necessary. That is what I did. I began to travel to my clients personally. I went to their local gyms or their homes. I even went to their local parks to provide my service to their children. There was no way I was willing to give up or give in to organizations that I felt did not realize or value my worth. I was not going to give up on my commitment to myself to go after my goals. I had to stay committed to my goals.

When you believe in yourself, your craft, your worth, and your work ethic, there will never be a reason for you to give up or settle. In life, no one is obligated to believe in you. Some people will believe in you while others will only believe in you after they see the rest of the world believe in you. After being boxed out of the first small scale training facility, the Boys & Girls Club and the largest sports complex in the country, I realized they were few who did not believe in me, but most importantly realized the majority of whom did believe in me. At that point, I knew I had to keep the believers believing, and then turn the non-believers into believers.

After a month of being away from the sports complex, they called me back and offered me the Head Basketball Director position. When I got that call, I knew I had the advantage and that they eventually realized my worth. But at that point, they could not afford me.

I was originally willing to work for them at a price less than my worth and quickly realized they did not appreciate my capabilities. When they decided to come back to renegotiate, my confidence to make it on my own had become so high that they could not afford to pay me for my services. Knowing that I put in so much work day after day and it was not appreciated helped make my work ethic unstoppable, but it also challenged me to stand firm in my own self-worth.

I hated it when someone did not believe in me or told me that there was something I could not do. It made me work even harder. I held myself to an extremely high standard, treated people with respect, and provided first-class service.

There was a time that I met with a man who was considered a communication guru. He helped entrepreneurs to promote their businesses and communicate with their target audiences. I met him after winning an elevator business pitch contest in 2013. When we started talking, he believed in me right off the bat. He challenged me and helped me break through my own comfort zone. He was about 6'5, 240lbs, karate guru, and an excellent businessman. Little did I realize that this man was insane.

During one of our meetings, he told me how he does a board breaking exercise to test entrepreneurs' willingness to break through any wall of adversity. I thought it was going to be a piece of cake because I saw people break boards on karate shows or movies all of the time. It was all good until he bought a thick board out right then and there. I instantly thought he was crazy, and there was no way I was willing to break my wrist, trying to impress this man, convincing him that I can break through a thick board. He taught me the technique and told me I had to break the board in order to move forward with our meetings and to gain the knowledge that he was willing to give me. When he had taught me the technique necessary to break the board, he gave me the thick board and told me to write something in the middle of the board that makes me so upset.

In the middle of the board, I wrote: "You CAN'T DO IT." I always hated it when someone told me I could not do something. Next, he held the board at me and told me to read it out loud to myself fifteen times. As I was saying the phrase, I grew so angry that I wanted to punch him instead of the board for making me tell myself that I could not do it. Out of nowhere, I used the technique he taught me and blasted through that thick board like a black belt karate guru. Once I looked at my wrist and saw it was still connected to my arm, but the board broke, I saw his smile. I knew that I could physically do anything I put my mind to at that time. This moment in life was a turning point that helped me realize that I could never give up or minimize my ability – no matter the circumstances.

Without a permanent job, I had a fear of being broke. I overcame it and started to generate a livable income. I learned that fear is only False Expectation Appearing Real. Putting in the work, having faith in God, and never giving up ensures there would never be a reason to have fear. I made excuses for why I needed to work for someone else, and then God confirmed that all I needed to do was keep my faith in Him. I tapped into my craft and stayed locked in on my mission. I realized I had to stop idolizing others and work so hard that others would learn to idolize me as a leader. I began to understand that if I did not go after my goals, then someone else would go after the same or similar goals and accomplish them, while I sit back and regret not going after my goals.

Another perfect example of why I never give in or give up is based upon the experiences of my barber since 2005, Darren Cobb. He was fortunate enough to tap into his craft of being a barber while he was still in high school. He cut hair in his fathers' basement and even traveled to people's homes. He slowly built a nice clientele of family and friends and quit the only real job he ever had. He was becoming a young entrepreneur, and without realizing it, he took his leap of faith. At that time, he would mess a few, well many customer's haircuts up, but not make them pay; he would be late from to time or even miss appointments altogether.

He did not do this purposely, but because he was young and not fully locked in on his mission. After a few years of cutting in his basement and traveling to people's homes, his work ethic and reputation for having magic hands allowed him the opportunity to level up and start cutting at the historic barbershop, "Just Kuttin' It Up." His mentor supported him based on his increased confidence and witnessed the work he put in. His mentor gave him a shot as a young barber looking to become an entrepreneur, which was a turning point for his life.

He continued to have faith in himself, becoming more consistent, learning to manage his time, and overcome adversity by raising his self-expectations and holding himself accountable. He provided a service based on integrity, confidence, and humility, and he is now arguably one of the best barbers in the Harrisburg community. Along his journey, he has lost friends, created a family, had to hustle and make adjustments, build his character, know his worth, and separate himself from the competition. Day after day, he had to make a conscious decision to embrace the calling over his life. He never took a break from cutting. He realized that if he did not cut, he and his family could not eat. He was not scared to take his leap of faith, although he had no clue where he was headed with being a barber. He just knew that if he cut day after day, that he would eventually become a master of his craft. He took his leap of faith before he was ready and has been flying high ever since.

I tell you these stories to help you understand that going after what you want, no matter what process you decide to endure, will require you to put in the work in order to see the results. You have the ability within you to be your own boss as long as you are not scared to tap into or maximize your worth. As long as you have faith in God, believe in yourself, continue working, and focus on how to make yourself a better person, you can achieve whatever goals you have in mind.

Reflecting on these truths, try to think of a time that you gave up and focus on how you felt. Pinpoint a time where you did not give up and why you did not. Be sure to write your reflection here and on the separate sheet used for the first six chapters as well.

HERE IS A TIME I GAVE UP, WHY I GAVE UP & HOW I FELT AFTER I GAVE UP

_____

_____

_____

_____

_____

_____

_____

_____

HERE IS A TIME I DID NOT GIVE UP, WHY I DID NOT GIVE UP & FEELING AFTER NOT GIVING UP

_____

_____

_____

_____

_____

_____

Chapter 7:

PREPARE WITH PURPOSE & PASSION

"The purposes of a person's heart are deep waters, but one who has insight draws them out" **Proverbs 20:5**

Preparing with purpose and passion is critical. Finding your purpose and passion for living is what makes you never want to give up or give less than 100% to win your day; to get one step closer to your ultimate goal. Your purpose and passion are based on your 'why' or 'what.' Why you matter, why you want to be successful, why you make certain decisions, what goals you want to achieve, what you're willing to sacrifice, and what process you are willing to endure are all questions that speak to the purpose. Without a clear idea of why you feel that you are chosen to be on earth, your goals will not be sufficient enough to motivate you. Purpose allows for your passion to be applied to your goals. Without a clear purpose, a person is less likely to become motivated or feel needed.

YOUR LIFE MATTERS

If no one ever told you that you matter, let me be the first to tell you that you matter! Your life is powerful, unique, special, productive, insightful, and one of a kind. I know that you have what it takes to manifest the greatness within you. It is possible and necessary that you acquire, work on, and develop your dreams. Too often, people believe that they do not matter and live with no purpose or passion, although it is something that is already inside of them. I am here to tell you that you do not have to settle for anything that you truly do not want because your life matters. In order for you to become successful, you must understand that you matter. Do not worry about those who do not think your life matters. When people disregard someone's life, it is most likely because, for them, their life does not matter. If you have a dream, you have to protect it against all naysayers.

If people cannot do something themselves, they are usually quick to tell someone they are not capable of that either. Think about all of the world heroes who realized that their lives mattered and did what was needed to make their dreams a reality:

Merry-Grace Majors, Andre Watson, Will Smith, Oprah Winfrey, Garrett Majors, Michael Jordan, Harriet Tubman, Marcus Burke, Malcolm X, Barack Obama, Anthony Atkinson, Westburn Majors, Russell Simmons, Chris Franklin, Martin Luther King, Muhammad Ali, Leland Nelson, Frederick Douglas, Jackie Robinson, Erich Majors, Maya Angelou, Johnny Bright, Wendell Scott, Rosa Parks, Langston Hughes. The list can go on for pages, but lastly, (insert your name). These are all people who understand that their life matters and are willing to do what it takes to make their life's purpose matter on earth.

When you are brave enough to take a stand and believe in yourself, that is when your ultimate purpose and passions will become evident. You may not know what you want to be quite yet, but if you believe you can become anybody you put your mind to, that is the first step. Once you believe, your ultimate purpose and passions will fall into place. All my life, I felt like I had a special connection with people who were already successful. I felt that special connection because I already knew that I was brave enough to not only watch their lives and dreams come true but brave enough to work towards my own dreams.

Every year in grade school during Black History Month, my teachers had my classes do reports on iconic African Americans in the world. In sixth grade, I did a project on Michael Jordan, the legendary NBA player. After this project, I told myself, people will research Bryan Majors, and I will be legendary for working towards and accomplishing my life long goals as well. I never had the excuse of not knowing anyone from my family, community, from my area or anything like that of why I could not attain my goals because they do exist. There are plenty of people in every profession who believed their life mattered enough to live their dreams. This means that you are fully capable of doing the same. From that project on, I knew that as long as I respected myself, stayed focused, working towards perfection, that one day some child will research my name and be inspired like I was inspired by Michael Jordan that day.

WHAT'S YOUR WHY?

When your life matters, your purpose, and passions will come into play, which will turn into your WHY. Your WHY will wake you up every morning. Your WHY will leave you with sleepless nights. Your WHY will get you back up after life knocks you down. Your WHY will not allow you to say no to your dreams. Your WHY will help you see your vision with a clear-eyed view. When you feel uncomfortable, your WHY will make you work to create a new comfort zone. My WHY has always been seeing my parents smile and for them to be proud of their youngest son. My parents invested so much in me that all I wanted to do was return their investment. My parents became my purpose and passion for living. I aim to reach success so bad so that they could reap the benefits. I appreciated how my mother and father shaped my life, so I worked relentlessly to show them instead of just tell them that I truly appreciate them.

My brothers are a part of my purpose and passion for living, so they can never want for anything as long as I live. My god-daughters are a part of my purpose and passion for living so that I can show them what to expect from a man. My mentors, the Harrisburg Community, Susquehanna University, Penn State, the believers and non-believers who invested their time in me are a part of my purpose and passion for living. Most importantly, when my father passed away, he fueled my purpose and passion for building Major Preparation. The morals and standards of Major Preparation are based upon the life skills my father taught so many young men before he was called to heaven. Major Preparation is why all my life I prepared with a purpose and passion. Major Preparation represents an idea. It represents a possibility. I thought that after my father passed that my life would be over. I could not imagine life without him. God allowed me to snap back into reality and use those trials and tribulations to turn inward to my purpose, passion, and way of life. I believed in myself, kept my faith in God, worked relentlessly, overcame adversity, and searched inside of myself all for that one moment of loss to slap me in the face and helped turn my purpose and passion into a reality.

Tragedy, in this case, helped me to truly focus on my passion and passing the lessons I have learned onto the world. Rather than remaining upset at what I thought God took from me, I focused on sharing all of the lessons that I was blessed to have learned from an amazing father. Helping others prepare for their lives has become my divine purpose and passion for life. Life will always be what you make it, not what other circumstances make of it, which is why you have to prepare with a purpose and passion. We all were created, destined, and born to be winners, and winning does not come from wishing but working - working towards what you believe in.

PURPOSE & PASSION

When you have an established purpose and passion, you have to love it unconditionally. Once you tap into your purpose and passion and truly care about it, it will groom you into the person you say you want to become. If you love your parents, you will make decisions to make them proud of you. If you love your goals, they will force you to make decisions to make your goals become a reality. When you are in love with your purpose and passion, you will learn to separate yourself from the losers and negative energy in your life. Having that unconditional love for your purpose and passion will make you invest in yourself and not want to let yourself down.

In life, you must have a purpose and passion driving you to success. You have to utilize all of your essential life skills to help you become successful. You have to understand that life is your story. Your purpose and passion will drive your storyline and dictate that what is most important in your life.

When all else fails or is achieved, you will have to look in the mirror and ask yourself if you are satisfied with your story. You have to embrace your purpose and passion for striving in your moment because you never know when your time will be up. That unconditional love for your purpose and passion will make you become consistent, confident, persistent, and you will grow to have no doubt in your mind that you will win in life.

You will believe that life is not over until you win. The only time you lose in life is when you quit. The Major Preparation theory is, either you win, or you learn. Losing is not a part of what we do. Losing is a mindset, not an action, or a result.

When you find that balance between purpose and passion, you will truly become a historic icon. Having the balance of purpose and passion will help you create an undeniable work ethic and the determination to become a champion in your own life. Having a purpose and passion in life will allow you to see your vision so clearly that it is bound to happen.

When you tap into your purpose and passion, then you have to instantly start your process. By starting your process, you have to think it, speak it, claim it, and go work for it. Having unconditional love for your purpose and passion kick-starts your process, and you have to have that same energy for your process to become successful. Life is a marathon, not a sprint, so it is important to start your process with the end in mind and have the perseverance to endure the longevity of your life's course.

As you work towards your goals, the best thing you can do is trust your process. Your process is for you. When you trust your process, that means you have unconditional faith in God's plan for what works for you.

When you are living in your process, you have to be faithful in it as if your life depends on how you perform day-to-day. While enduring your process, you cannot give up, you have to act on your daily goals, you have to take charge of your destiny, and most importantly you cannot quit during the process. Yes, the process will be challenging, and it will make you think enough is enough.

The process will make you feel like you have no more energy left. The process will frustrate you and make you uncomfortable. All of those emotions will become justifiable if you want your end goal bad enough. If you believe in yourself and if you are willing to put in the work, in the long run, you will see the manifestation of your dreams.

The only person who can knock you off of your square from enduring your process is you. You knock yourself off your square when you become comfortable, when you get satisfied, when you get complacent and when you give in to the adversity. In my process with Major Preparation, I have no doubt in my mind that I will reach the goals for the company. I work hard day after day. I use my time wisely. I turned my pain into greatness to push me to where I am and where I plan to go. I know that my pain will be a part of my prize. I challenge myself day by day to win. I know that what I did last week has become irrelevant, that what I do each and every day is what matters.

My plan is to leave this earth and accomplish everything I set out to achieve with no excuses. No day is promised, and I know that by the end of each day, I maxed out my will and drive to win that day of the process. In my process, I am determining my own future. I have the capability to choose my own future because I understand that I have the power to succeed in life and achieve the goals I strive toward. I am open to new opportunities. I found what I love to do and work at it daily. I stay away from things that are future killers like dropping out of school, doing drugs, getting involved with negative groups, or wasting time. I stay positive, and I know I will be successful. I want you to know that you are and can be successful.

When I was born, I knew I was born a chooser. I am a chooser because I have the power to choose to make good or bad choices.
Lastly, every day I go confidently in the direction of my dreams. I live the life I have imagined because I said YES to my goals, to my potential, to my work ethic, to my determination, to my drive, and to my purpose and passion. All you have to do is say YES to your purpose and passion.

LOCKED IN

As you are locked into your purpose and passion, YOU will have to make sacrifices that those who are not locked into the purpose or passions yet will not be willing to make or understand. If you are planning on being an athlete, focus on your sport. If you are planning on being a doctor, focus and learn from other great doctors. If you are planning to become a president of the country, focus and learn from other presidents. If you want to become an astronaut, then research astronauts. You have to stay focused on your goal. There will be plenty of times you cannot go to the party because you are reading or listening to topics related to your goals instead. You will not always be able to go to the movies because you need to be in the gym working out. You will not listen to the negative music that is popular because you would rather listen to Les Brown, Eric Thomas, David Shands, Inky Johnson or Bryan Majors' motivational messages.

When you are enduring your process, you will have to become a full-time player and active participant in your own growth and development. Full-time player means no days off striving to become the person you plan to become. I am not saying you do not enjoy yourself with friends and family, but I am saying you have to work before play, and you have to keep your priorities first. When you are locked into your process, whatever needs to be done daily needs to be done before you decide to go do anything that is not on task. It is important that you have your purpose and passion aligned, take personal responsibility, develop good life habits, and have the courage to set yourself up to be successful during your process.

Personal responsibility means being accountable for your actions and decisions, as well as the positive and negative consequences of them. Taking personal responsibility is to have control over or be in charge of your process and not to live an unfocused life while developing good life habits to help you evolve and avoid potential barriers to your success.

Good life habits are patterns of behaviors that are gained through your repetition and practice. Lastly, personal responsibility means having the courage to set yourself up for success and not get stuck. Having that courage means you are able to face difficult situations or circumstances in spite of fear or excuses. Preparing with a purpose and passion is going to grow to become the reason why you will never fail at reaching the pot of gold at the end of the rainbow.

Now is the time where you pull that sheet of paper back out, take the pledge, and create your eleven reasons why you will not fail at life despite the adversity that you face or have to overcome.

I (insert your name) _____, say yes to my life and will not fail!!

11 REASONS WHY I WILL NOT FAIL

1. _____
   _____

2. _____
   _____

3. _____
   _____

4. _____
   _____

5. _____
   _____

6. _____
   _____

7. _____
   _____

8. _____
   _____

9. _____
   _____

10. _____
    _____

11. _____
    _____

Chapter 8:

PREPARE YOURSELF TO GO HARDER THAN YOU EVER IMAGINED:

"For God did not give us a spirit of timidity, but a spirit of power, of love and of self-discipline." **2 Timothy 1:7**

Preparing yourself to go harder than you ever imagined is the next level of the journey after you have your purpose, passion, and process aligned. As you prepare for this step, it is essential that you seize your opportunity, run your race, allow yourself room for mistakes, stay grounded, work on your process and go hard enough to attain your highest and truest expression of yourself. Your life is what you make it! You have the option to sit back and allow life to play the cards you are dealt with by default or rise to the occasion and play the hand the way you would want it to be played.

SEIZE YOUR OPPORTUNITY

Seizing your opportunity comes from your own preparation process. Day-to-day, you have to Train For Triumph and prepare you for your destiny. Every day you should be going through or reading something that will enlighten your mindset and help you prepare for your destiny. I remember my childhood best friend, Gilbert Brown, who has played division one basketball at the University of Pittsburgh. He was one of the star players on his team and in the Big East. He had aspirations of going to the NBA, had a great collegiate career and did everything he thought possible in order to be drafted into the NBA to further his basketball career. He trained non-stop when the season was over while he was in Pittsburgh and when he was home, he would call me to train him to keep him sharp for when he had to go to NBA team tryouts. His agent believed he would get drafted, he was on the ESPN list of top players and all, but it was not what God had planned for him at the time.

It was NBA draft night, we had a draft party at his parent's house, and we sat side by side and watched the entire draft. Pick after pick went by, various calls from his agent came through saying that teams were interested in him, he watched players who he felt were not better than he get drafted.

It was the last round with a few picks left when his agent called back and said that he should be picked up within the last few picks of the draft. The last few picks came, and he was still not drafted. We looked at each other for about eight seconds before either of us said a word. I then told him, "Bro, we just have to work hard to turn these non-believers into believers." He replied, "You damn right!" That became a turning point in his life, he did not quit or give up on his goals, but he continued to work out, go to tryouts and was blessed enough to receive a call from the Boston Celtics, where he was eventually picked up as a free agent. He played throughout the pre-season, and then eventually got cut from the team. Once again, he did not give up or give in to the adversity that he had to face. His agent helped him receive a contract to play professional basketball overseas, where he has been a professional basketball player for the past eight years.

Every moment you live, you have to embrace all change and use it as preparation so that when it is your time to perform your craft on a big-time stage, you can seize the opportunity. Gilbert is making a great living for himself and his family, still working towards becoming an NBA player but taking full advantage of being a professional basketball player overseas. He did not get discouraged based because he didn't make it to the NBA. It was just not his destiny at the time. As long as he keeps working and staying focused on his goals; if the NBA is meant to be along his journey, it will happen. He never had the thought of giving up or giving in because basketball is his purpose and passion. He impacts other lives with his story and challenges, along with being able to provide assistance for his family and friends. He is successful because he was courageous enough to live his professional basketball dreams and seize his opportunity.

RUN YOUR RACE

As you prepare to go harder than you ever imagined, you also have to run your race. Understand that what is for you is for you and you alone. What you go through as you pursue your goals is meant for you to endure to help your own personal development. All my life, I decided to live the right way, and it seemed like my end goal was always so far away. I did not realize that maintaining and being consistent was building my reputation, my work ethic, my drive, my determination, my character, my integrity, my personality, and my story. I look back at high school friends who wanted everything at that moment and did whatever they could to get it. They went and got what they wanted at the time illegally, had a great time living their race, but unfortunately, they had no idea they were blocking their own blessings on their race to success. Some friends were in a better life with financial and materialistic trappings in high school than now as an adult. On my end, I ran my race in a way that I would win consistently - daily for the rest of my life.

As a basketball player, I had a hard time understanding that I have to run my own race. I always felt that I was the best point guard on any court I stepped on. I played against, defended, and beat some big-time players who ended up going on to play Division One collegiate basketball (which I always wanted to play) while I played Division Three basketball. I struggled, dealing with that until I realized that my journey is my own, and I had to run my own race in life. I had to stop comparing my blessings to others, my success to others and focus on my success and how I can inspire others to reach their success. When my career was over, I accomplished accolades that a lot of those guys never came close to on the court and in the classroom. I had to stop focusing on their race and make sure I was the fastest running my own race.

Once I locked into what my collegiate career was supposed to be, there was no stopping me. I realized that the energy I was using to compare my race to anyone else's race was taking away from my race. When I focused on my race, I gained a sense of self-worth. I realized what I was accomplishing day after day and how I could impact the lives of others by living my race. I learned to apply myself limitlessly. I learned to talk less and grind more. I learned not to wait or wish for anything but to work for it. I had the confidence to become an uncommon breed and set a new standard for living and running life's race. I started to envision myself as an icon, as a legendary man who changed the world, and as a man many would be inspired by because I lived my dreams, not my fears.

ALLOW YOURSELF ROOM FOR MISTAKES

In life, the goal is to always get to your next level of success. The earlier you focus on your own race in life, the more room you have to make mistakes. Many people are scared to take their leap of faith or run their own race. By the time they gain courage, too many feel as though it is too late. When I finally took my leap of faith, yes, I was scared. I was turning twenty-four years old. However, once I took that leap, it was the best feeling in the world - taking my last $1,500 in my account and investing it into my goals. I knew that I had to make it, or else I would be broke.

I knew I had my vision, purpose, and passion all lined up but was unsure what was going to be next. I just believed enough in God and myself that I would figure out my next move. I then bought a few t-shirts from A.C. Moore, took them to a local print shop and had my logo put on t-shirts. When I received the shirts back, I was prepared to give them away to a few local celebrities I knew, explain my vision, purpose, and passion to them in order to get their reaction. Their reactions were not going to break me, but I was ready for whatever their feedback was going to be. I got a great response from the majority, and then, of course, did not get a good response from a few, which was perfectly fine with me. I would sell shirts out of my mother's basement to my family and friends. I then loaded up my trunk with t-shirts, drove all around the city, parked and popped my trunk, then would sell my t-shirts with a brochure of the Major Preparation vision, purpose, and passion in different neighborhoods.

Initially, I only sold the shirts for $10, not realizing I was only making a three-dollar profit when I should have been charging $15-$20 a shirt. I was just happy that people invested their hard-earned money into my brand, even though I ended up losing more money than I was making. After the buzz of the shirts was around the city, I raised the price to $15. At that point, I started being able to recycle the profit. I eventually grew to where I could charge $20-$25 per shirt based upon the reputation and others believing in the brand. I gave myself room to grow and learn from my experiences. I did not have to reinvent the wheel of learning how to market my brand or my vision. I studied the race of Nike, Under Armor, and Adidas brands all took to make their companies what they are today. Their vision, purpose, or passion was no different than what I have for Major Preparation. I realized that if they could do it, then I definitely could as well. No goals or dreams are built overnight. They are built over time. The more time you give yourself to build, the greater the chance you have to reach the finish line in your race for success. Time is one of the most important phenomena in life that you do not get back, so you have to maximize every second of your life.

STAY GROUNDED

As you prepare to go harder in life, you will grow, and your goals will become clearer. You will begin to fully understand the small victories and appreciate them. When you appreciate the days of small beginnings or victories, you will learn to stay grounded when you accomplish bigger victories. This goes back to the idea of remaining humble throughout the process. I remember when I bought my very first car. I was a sophomore in college and saved all of my work-study checks up to buy this car.

The car cost $1,500.00. It was a 2000 green Dodge Intrepid with tint and a banging system in the trunk. I thought I was big time! I was so excited about having a car and being able to go where I wanted when I wanted but was not prepared to maintain a car.

I did not take into consideration having to get tune-ups, oil changes, paying for gas, keeping my car clean, and understanding the importance of treating my Dodge Intrepid like it was a Rolls Royce, my dream car. I was driving on my way home from college when the car started shaking, I started smelling smoke, and the steering wheel locked up on me while I was in the middle of the highway. I was lucky enough not to have any cars around me, and I went right into panic mode and pulled the car over. I called my parents to ask them what happened and asked what I should do. I then called AAA, who came to check my car out and they stated my engine blew because I never got an oil change or tune-up since I purchased the 'whip.'

My car did not have any oil in it for months. When I got the car, I did not appreciate the blessing. I got arrogant and felt like I did not need anyone for transportation anymore. Well, I learned from then on to always remain grounded because what you have today can be gone today, let alone tomorrow. I not only lost my car, but I lost my hard-earned $1,500.00 as well. I was later fortunate enough to work towards having new cars and know the importance of treating what I have with the utmost care, cleanliness, and appreciation so that when I can get that Rolls Royce, I will know how to cherish it.

WORK ON YOUR WORK

When you are going harder than you ever imagined, you will learn to unswervingly 'work on your work.' To 'work on your work' means to always create a new comfort zone for yourself. As you are going after your goals, the moment you get comfortable is the moment you put your own barriers in front of you that you have to overcome. Life itself will put barriers on your path for you to figure out how to overcome, get around, or breakthrough, so do not put your own barriers up. Every day, it is necessary that you learn something new, that you listen to something motivational and that you accomplish a new victory. It is essential that you remember all of your victories add to your life story.

You never know when God will call you home, so whenever that time comes, be sure that at that moment, your life can be an inspiration to someone else. If you get to the point that your work ethic is allowing you to accomplish all of your goals with no problem, then you need to raise your level of thinking, become more creative, and determine how you can continue to get better and become more successful, impacting even more lives.

I got to the point where I worked hard enough to get to a certain point within growing my brand that I got extremely comfortable. I got stagnant, and I did not feel that I had continued growth. During that time, I sought out motivational messages. I heard Les Brown talk about asking for help and investing in a life coach. I thought Les Brown was crazy. I did not know why Les Brown needed a life coach because he was one of the best, if not the best, motivational speakers in the world. It then hit me. Michael Jordan had Phil Jackson as his coach, Tiger Woods had a golf coach, Shawn Lewis had Destry Mangus, and even Barack Obama had a mentor or life coach.

I had to learn that you can only go so far, working on your work on your own. I had my own life coaches in line, including my parents and mentor, but I did not have a goal coach. I thought of the term goal coach because my life was already becoming everything I thought it would be, but having someone else hold me accountable for certain goal guidelines would help me become even more efficient.

By the grace of God, my goal coach was someone who has been watching me build since I took my leap of faith. I was at a college fair for students at Harrisburg High School, and there she was. She was a vendor for the students, but when she saw me, it was like God sent her there specifically for me. This lady has always been on point with her life, I knew her for years, and she asked me a few questions about my goals that I could not answer, which she had the solution for.

From there on, I knew she would be the perfect goal coach for me. She is the same one who gave me the spark I needed to write this book that you are reading right now. She first told me, "B, you aren't that hot anymore!" I looked at her like she was insane, thinking, "I am B.Maj. I've always been hot!" She challenged me to write this book in three months. She challenged me and got me out of my comfort zone. She didn't realize I was already locked into my purpose and passion. I emailed her my complete rough draft in 28 days. She was in awe. She called me and said, "Yo! You are freaking nuts! I never witnessed anybody do what you just did!" I just smirked and thought, "You don't know who you are messing with!" I replied, "I am one of God's gifts. I can do anything I put my mind to!" As you prepare to go harder than you ever imagined, many will respect your work and be willing to help you continue your race and push you to greatness.

When you work on your work, your maturity as a person will grow rapidly, which will allow you to go from running to sprinting while Training For Triumph. Your personal accountability level will rise, meaning you will be accountable for your actions and not need others to hold you accountable for what you are supposed to do. Your leadership characteristics will never go unnoticed, so when someone mentions your name, and you are not in the room, you will still receive the utmost respect. Always 'work on your work.' Never settle for less than your worth.

ATTAIN YOUR HIGHEST
& TRUEST EXPRESSION OF YOURSELF

The end goal of preparing yourself to go harder than you ever imagined should be to attain your highest and truest expression of yourself. Your life has to matter enough for you to try your best to endure the longevity of success instead of short-term gratification.

The older you become, the wiser and more experienced you should become. The quest for the highest and truest expression of yourself should always be chased but never attained. We should always pursue who we are, but know that we are constantly growing and evolving until the last day we serve on earth. Your highest and truest expression of yourself should be so high that you can never get complacent with who you are. It is great to go hard and reach levels of success but never stop striving to reach perfection, which is impossible, but you can strive to #BeMajor.

The task is to set goals so high that you have to constantly reinvent yourself and evolve. We can never obtain perfection, but the process to get there is filled with growth and wisdom.

The time you take to reflect on your growth during your race in life is essential. Just be mindful not to rest so much that you get comfortable resting. You can always do more. As you strive to attain your personal highest and truest self, do not be afraid to ask questions. Understand that there are people who did everything you plan to do already extremely well. Therefore, you do not have to reinvent the wheel. Simply research it or ask for the blueprint. The worst thing you can do is try to become successful or reach your peak by yourself.

As a basketball trainer, I have clients who work consistently on their work by coming to me to help them prepare for their basketball journey. The preparation these players go through allows them to strive and attain their highest and truest expressions when the preparation meets the moment. There is a young player by the name of Malia Tate-Defreitas, who was one of my first clients ever. She is, by far, the most unbelievable girl I have ever trained. In high school, she scored over 3,500 points, won two state champion titles, and earned a Division 1 scholarship. While in college, she scored over 1,000 points in just two years. Her preparation process was so real that when the moments met her process, she made the moments look easy to endure.

Another player who has been one of my long-term clients is Chris Whitaker. Chris is a special kid, and he has extreme confidence in me to help prepare him for his life journey of success on and off the court. I have just as much confidence in him. He became a little brother to me like I am to my mentor, Shawn Lewis. The relationship between Chris and me has become so close because of the standard I hold him to and the way he relies on me to help him become the person and player he wants to become. We talked more about life skills than basketball.

His talent is going to take him far, but his mentality and work ethic is what is going to make him become legendary. There were times when workouts were over, and Chris had to make situational based free throws in order to complete the workouts. Chris would miss time after time when he first started training with me. He eventually grew to the point he would endure the workouts and finish his free throw series with no problem. Chris was a player who was outright talented but needed his work ethic to match his talents in order for him to attain his highest and truest expression of himself. After some time, he prepared and developed into arguably one of the best players in the state during his tenure as a Harrisburg Cougar.

During a legendary game in Harrisburg, the preparation met the moment, and Chris overcame that moment. The game was in overtime with one second left on the clock, and Chris' team was down by two points. Chris caught the court length pass turned and shot the three-point shot to win the game and got fouled. Chris was awarded three foul shot attempts, nailed all three free-throw attempts, and won the game for his team. After Chris hit the last shot, he ran to his grandmother and father to embrace them. He then found me, and we embraced each other. I was extremely proud of Chris because when the preparation met his moment, he could seize the moment and attain his highest and truest expression of himself. All he could say was, "MAJOR WORK = MAJOR RESULTS!!!!!"

Chapter 9:

PREPARE MENTALLY, PHYSICALLY, SPIRITUALLY & EMOTIONALLY FOR SUCCESS

"I have set the LORD always before me. Because he is at my right hand, I will not be shaken." **Psalm 16:8**

PREPARING MENTALLY

Preparing mentally is basically setting your foundation. Mentally, you have to take on the challenge of having stability in your thoughts and behaviors. Having mental stability is being able to control how you think, feel, behave, act, and react to life. Becoming successful is based upon your own personal will, drive, determination, and faith. These are all things you can control. I take pride in reading the Serenity Prayer daily:

God grant me the Serenity to accept the things I cannot change. Courage to change the things I can and Wisdom to know the difference.

This prayer is essential to my life because it reinforces that you, as a person, can only rely on God to put you through and pull you through life's situations. You do have the capability to think positive, feel positive, behave positive, act positive, and react positive just the way God would always want. Of course, God will not have everything go your way, but understand that God gives his toughest battles to his toughest soldiers. When life gets hard, realize that the pain is not here to stay, but just to pass and your reward for overcoming the pain will be beyond measure. The way you think reflects how you feel. The way you feel reflects how you act. The way you act reflects how you react. It is up to you to do so in a positive manner in order to #BeMajor. Many times, I am asked how I am always so positive. The answer is simple; I am in control of my mental stability.

Think Major + Act Major = BeMajor

PREPARING PHYSICALLY

Preparing physically is another level of your personal development and structure. Personally, I strive to be in the best shape of my life every day of my life. I love to look good and feel good each and every day because I do not take any day for granted.

My father made sure as a child that my brothers and I always were active in sports and did our pushups, sit-ups, toe touches, and squats so that we could endure life's long journey to success. When my father was in his prime, he was built like Superman, strong as an ox and tall. He looked like he could conquer the world at any moment.

My father instilled the physical work ethic in my brothers and me at an early age, and I never wanted to lose the body build and frame that I worked so hard to obtain. My father gave me the analogy that my body is like any dream car that I could possibly want. My dream car is a Rolls Royce, so I had to treat my body like it was a Rolls Royce. I had to feed it properly, keep it tuned up, and had to keep it functioning. I never could put toxic gas into my body. Those reasons are why I take pride in working out consistently, staying in shape, and never doing drugs. Along your journey to success, you will have a lot of adversity to break through, so your body has to be able to withstand the fight. If you are not physically fit to endure the fight, there will come a time where you get knocked down, and you will feel like you will not be able to bounce back. I am not saying you have to go become the next bodybuilder, but be able to be in enough shape that fits your lifestyle and give you the capability to live a healthy lifestyle. I personally want to be in a Rolls Royce. I know when I do get my Rolls Royce, I will look good stepping out of it, so I work relentlessly in the gym to stay in shape.

Physically, besides looking good while getting out of my future Rolls Royce, I am preparing for long-term success. Long-term success has a great deal of advantages. Having long-term success goals will create generational wealth. Your long-term success can be the focal point for a child twenty years after you have been called to heaven. Long-term success is not easy, but surely attainable if you are physically fit enough to maintain your legacy.

PREPARING SPIRITUALLY

Spiritually - it is vital that you stay faithful to whatever religion you believe in. You will hit peaks in your life when you have no idea in the world why certain situations may happen to you in your life. I am here to tell you that what happens in your life is meant to become a turning point in your life. If you feel as though something is going wrong, turn it into a positive. If something is positive, turn it into another positive. Do not rest on sorrows or soak in accomplishments. Preparing spiritually requires you to have a sense of heightened reverence to a higher power.

Spiritually, when you are fully connected in your religion is when total blessings pour in like a waterfall. Being fully locked into your religion is a choice that you have to make in your own life. No one can tell you when, but you will eventually go through something that being locked completely into your religion will be your only option. Just always prepare with ultimate faith in whomever you believe in. I personally believe in God. I know that He is my rock. I know that He has His hands on my life, and I am extremely blessed to be a son of His. The blessings that have come my way have been mind-blowing from staying faithful to Him.

PREPARING EMOTIONALLY

Your emotional state of mind is critical to your endurance, along with your life long journey to success. Success is wonderful if you are emotionally prepared for it. Realize that with success comes a great deal of responsibility. You are not only responsible for yourself but for your family, friends, community, and everyone who considers you a role model. You have to be emotionally stable enough to endure the hatred that comes along with success, the reliability that comes along with success, and the attention that comes along with success.

On your journey to success, not everyone will be a fan of what you are doing. Some will try to say or do things to bring you down, but you have to stay emotionally strong enough to block them out and not give in to negative energy. When you encounter negative energy, stay strong: do not even acknowledge it. Taking time to acknowledge negative energy takes time away from your positive energy.

As you reach new levels of success, family, friends, communities, and others will try to put extra stress on you to fulfill their needs. It will be on you to stay emotionally stable enough to say 'yes' to what makes you feel comfortable and 'no' to what does not. You are not obligated to partake in situations just because you are asked to do so. There will be plenty of times that you give and provide for others that will go unnoticed by many, but your good deeds will not go unnoticed by God. The moment you do say 'no' - expect people to criticize you. Do not lose your stable emotional state of mind. People criticize Michael Jordan, Kobe Bryant, Jay Z, Bill Gates, Oprah Winfrey, Malcolm X, Michelle, and Barack Obama all for being courageous enough to become who they set out to be, so expect others to criticize you as well.

Chapter 10:

PREPARE FOR YOUR FUTURE WITH BACK UP PLANS:
FROM A-Z:

"For I know the thoughts that I think toward you, says the LORD,
thoughts of peace and not of evil, to give you a future and a hope."
Jeremiah 29:11

Preparing for your future with back up plans from A-Z means that there should never be a time in your life that you are not doing something that you love or are passionate about because you have twenty-six back up plans. Having an ultimate goal is essential. The backup plans are not far off your ultimate goals, but different avenues to always keep you connected with your ultimate goal. For my life, my back-up plans are what keep me able to be versatile enough to adapt and adjust to any environment or circumstances. For every plan, there should be more than one avenue to which you can reach your ultimate goal. Furthermore, it is important to have multiple back-up plans in case one dream does not become a reality.

My ultimate goal was to become an NBA Player, to play the game I loved, give back to others, and support my family. I feel as though I truly gave everything I had to make that ultimate goal become a reality. I had to make adjustments in how to do what I loved, give back to others, and support my family. Here is my back up plan that I created when I was a sophomore in college and still working through today.

MAJOR PREP BACKUP PLANS SO I ALWAYS BECOME SUCCESSFUL

A.   Start My Own Sports Development Training Company
B.   Become a High School Basketball Coach
C.   Become a College Basketball Coach
D.   Become an Athletic Director
E.   Become a Motivational Speaker
F.   Become a Clothing Designer
G.   Become a Commentator
H.   Start My Own Non-Profit Organization
I.   Write A Book about life
J.   Become an NBA Agent
K.   Become an NBA General Manager

L.   Become a Professional Basketball Scout
M.   Become a Fitness Personal Trainer
N.   Become a Referee
O.   Become a Teacher
P.   Become a Principal
Q.   Become a Business Consultant
R.   Become Mayor of Harrisburg
S.   Work For Nike
T.   Basketball Training Complex
U.   Boys and Girls Club Director
V.   Never Give up
W.   Always Make My Mom Proud
X.   If I Get This Far, It's All Bad
Y.   You Are Full of Crap
Z.   Just pitiful if you have to rely on Z!

Your back up plans should always align with your ultimate goal. Sometimes in life, no matter how hard you work towards a goal that you think is for you, it may not be what God has planned for you. He may be preparing you for an even greater goal. If you do not know what you want to be yet, or what backup plans work for you, it could be you have to try different things and see what works for you and what does not. You have to be flexible and open to different avenues of life.

Being able to master different trades only maximizes your worth and will help you reach different peaks of your life. The world's richest people have 5-8 streams of income, so you have to be knowledgeable and willing to tap into different avenues in order to create an extremely wealthy lifestyle for yourself. In short, we all need a hustle, and it is necessary to have more than one trick up your sleeve in case life's circumstances change your course of action.

Here is a time for you to take a few minutes to write down your own set of back up plans or different avenues for you to always become successful based on your ultimate goals.

MY BACKUP PLANS TO ALWAYS BECOME SUCCESSFUL

A._____

B._____

C._____

D._____

E._____

F._____

G._____

H._____

I._____

J._____

K._____

L._____

M._____

N._____

O._____

P._____

Q._____

R._____

S._____

T._____

U._____

V._____

W._____

X._____

Y._____

Z._____

Chapter 11:

PREPARE FOR SUCCESS, WHICH IS A JOURNEY OF PERSISTENCE AND PERSEVERANCE IN SPITE OF FAILURE:

"Fight the good fight of faith; take hold of the eternal life to which you were called, and you made the good confession in the presence of many witnesses." **1 Timothy 6:12**

As you prepare with persistence and perseverance, in spite of failure, understand that you will grow to become unstoppable and undeniable. You must always make sure that you are improving yourself. You have to continuously amaze those who follow your lead and push yourself to the limit and then more. Your persistence and perseverance, in spite of failure, comes down to your own will and determination when it is all said and done. You have what it takes to become legendary and be whoever you set your mind to become. You do not need anyone else to believe in you as long as you believe in yourself. If no one told you before, let me be the first to tell you that I believe in you! If you get denied one time, you have to try again. If you get denied a second time, then go back for the third and so on and so forth. Not everyone will believe in you right away, but as long as you stay persistent and persevere, you will come across the right people to help you get to where you want to go.

In this world, there are no handouts. As cold as it seems, you cannot live as if becoming successful will come easy. Some people reach their success after one, two, three, twenty, thirty, or forty years of working towards it. You have to embrace your journey and not anyone else's. There is no timeline that can be shifted outside of what God wants you to accomplish within a given time. Understand that God will reveal things to you when you have worked your way into the skills and discipline needed to handle the next level. God never makes mistakes. He only gives glory to those with a story. Everyone's story is different, just like their glory. But your glory can be everything you want it to be if you go through your Major Preparation process. Trusting the process is one thing, but making sure you are ready for the next level is the biggest lesson of all. If an opportunity comes to you, but you are not ready for it, it's almost as pointless as a missed opportunity. We must strive to always be working and ready to answer the call, regardless of when it comes through.

Here are a few questions that I need you to answer as we wrap up. Write these questions down on the sheet of paper along with all of the other notes that you collected from the previous chapters.

1. Do you want to be a leader or a follower?
2. Do you want to be the head or tail"?
3. Do you want to be a champion or a chump?
4. Do you have what it takes to accomplish your goals?
5. Do you want your destiny to be in your own hands or the system's hands?

THEN DON'T GET BORED, GET BETTER!

ALWAYS PREPARE WITH PERSISTENCE & PERSEVERANCE!

ALWAYS TRAIN FOR TRIUMPH & REMEMBER

MAJOR WORK FOR MAJOR RESULTS!

CONCLUSION

I greatly appreciate you taking the time to read this book. This book is the start of a lifestyle that will impact not only you but the entire world. The plan is to help everyone in the world to become prepared in order to live a Major Prep Lifestyle despite his or her circumstances. There is no reason that we are not in control of our futures. There are too many youths of all races in the criminal systems. There are too many people working jobs they do not love. There are way too many youths on street corners, and there are not enough people living their goals, which will inspire others to live their goals.

I am asking that you take the pledge to live your goals and apply the Major Prep Lifestyle in your life. I am asking you to recognize the qualities of positive leadership and to strive to incorporate those qualities in yourself. I am asking that you act with honesty and sincerity, always doing what is right. I am asking you to realize that we cannot always change a situation; however, we can control our reaction to that situation. I am asking you to learn to win and learn with humility. We can often accomplish more with the help of others that we can on our own because to be successful, you need good teammates. I am asking you to understand that effective communication is essential.

I am asking you to understand the importance of treating all people and their belongings as you want to be treated. I am asking you to first and foremost understand that you are valuable, and you have to take care of yourself, your belongings, and your community. I am asking you to accept that respect is earned, and that to be respected, you must treat others with equal respect.

I am asking you to understand that to be successful in life, it takes major work, energy, and a commitment to doing your best and finishing what you started. Realize you have the ability to dedicate yourself to your goals and complete them no matter how difficult the course may be or what adversities you have to overcome. I am asking you to learn to choose friendships/relationships with those that share values and goals that you respect and who, in turn, respect your values and goals. I am asking you to live a Major Prep Lifestyle.

I am asking you to review your personal workbook that we created and put it in a place you will see daily. Take a picture of it and email it to me so I can hold you accountable. I am asking you to commit to greatness!

Please contact me via email to send me your workbook creation and your feedback about Training For Triumph. Majorprepllc@gmail.com

MAJOR PREPARATION: TESTIMONIALS

I have known Bryan for over ten years. Over the years, I have been a coach, trainer & mentor to Bryan; I consider him my little brother. I have watched him grow from a hard-working young man to an even harder working man. His passion and drive to want to be successful is very inspiring. His motivation to want to help people is evident in his everyday life. Bryan and his Major Prep movement has motivated and inspired many other people, young and old, and me to always put in Major Work for Major Results. **Shawn Lewis – Hard 2 Guard Sports Performance Training**

Hungry. Never Satisfied. Always bettering his best. I could go on and on, but I want to let you know, if you have "Putting in Major Work for Major Results" in your hands, you already have a competitive advantage! You are learning lessons from a man that graduated with his master's in public administration then, an hour later, wore his graduation cap and gown to a business plan competition - and won! Read this book and, more importantly, apply the lessons daily to Get Major Results! **Leland J. Nelson, President Dirty Dog Hauling, LLC**

Bryan Majors has inspired a new day in leadership! Inspiration, enthusiasm, determination, and preparation are all words that immediately come to mind. The millennial generation is in desperate need of a new wave of leaders who can inspire, connect, and effectively communicate in a way the reaches their core. Bryan Majors is on a lifelong mission, and nothing will stop him from impacting our future leaders of America. **Rashaan Carlton, Director of Athletics Penn State Harrisburg**

You keep soaring! With your feet planted firmly on the ground but never standing still. I think this Major Prep Lifestyle is amazing. **Mark Hawthorne, Boys & Girls Club Program Director**

Your energy and enthusiasm for helping others is truly inspirational. You definitely practice what you preach... Major Work=Major Results!! I look forward to seeing how far you can and will go. Best of luck. **Dale Fallon, Communication Gym**

Bryan Majors is one of the most prolific and unforgettably dynamic young individuals I know. I met Bryan during the AACCCP business plan pitch competition, where he slid into the podium like a batter running towards home plate, all dressed in cap and gown, arriving last minute because he was graduating college. Although the competition was great, Bryan delivered the award-winning pitch, confidently embossing his brand on the audience and taking home the grand prize. That day and each day, I've encountered him since has been no less inspiring. **Shariah Brown, AACCCP, Chair**

Bryan and my brotherhood grew from a common goal of wanting to help others and lead by example. While speaking about his mission, I saw that he also subscribed to the idea that the world lacks young men, like us, who have learned from life's lessons and are ready to pay it forward to our own communities. The genuine nature of our brotherhood was seamless, as if he was a 'brother from another mother.' I volunteered my skills in website development and design to the already growing production of Major Prep products and brand. Major Prep is regarded as more than branding in material but in one's lifestyle. I'm honored to be part of the team. **Timothy White, Jr. - Successful Ex-Offender & Program Coordinator at Amiracle4sure**

FAMILY

When you meet Bryan Majors...you meet Major Prep! Bryan is the living, breathing embodiment of a young Black man whose daily life says he is putting in Major Work to get Major Results - SUCCESS!!! Bryan is unselfishly dedicated to the community and helping others to see and bring out the Greatness in themselves - physically, mentally, spiritually. Bryan's vision for Major Prep was fueled by the challenges he encountered as a young high school basketball point guard with his coach and the experience of his father's death at the end of his sophomore year in college. The degree of perseverance he exhibited to walk through those events and come out on the 'positive' side, led him to understand the importance of faith, training, lectures, studying his craft so that he could dig down deep inside, grab that internal fortitude, and move on with life. He learned that he was being PREPARED every day of his life ....and that if you PREPARE....you will get Major Results.

Why do I know all of this? I'm his mom, and I know his journey. His journey is real, and he is committed to helping people of all ages, races, capabilities, understand how they, too, can have successful life journeys despite the odds.

Bryan is a great man! I love him because he is my son, but I like him because he is a man of character who is true to his word, genuinely cares for people, and has the head and heart of a servant leader. Merry-Grace Majors, Mother

Bryan has an infectious energy that you can't help but get excited about when he's around. Seeing the work that my baby brother puts into everything he does is an inspiration to me. Years of blood, sweat, and tears towards achieving his goals and seeing them beginning to manifest is amazing. He pushes people past what they may have been able to see in themselves. Keep shining your light bro and encouraging others,

especially the youth, to do the same. I know Dad is looking over you and beeping his horn in excitement for you.
Westburn Majors, Brother

Bryan is someone who has an impact on people of all ages. His ability to be a leader is incredible. He has such a strong connection to the community, and anyone he comes in contact with that he will be known as one of the greats. He inspires, he motivates, and he uplifts as I've never seen before. He is a hero to many people and emphasizes that in any aspect of life, you have to put in Major Work to get Major Results. When you think of Bryan, greatness comes to mind.
Garrett Majors, Brother

Bryan Majors is Major Prep. To me, Major Prep is a lifestyle that's dedicated to 11 Key Principles. If you read his book, you will learn about them. I apply these principles to my everyday life, which helps me to be MAJOR. Bryan Majors is my twin brother, and with God, family, friends, and incorporating the Major Prep 11 key principles, I am on a path of success. Erich Majors, Pennsylvania State Trooper, Brother

Bryan Majors is a tremendous leader and mentor! His dedication and motivation for succeeding is contiguous to anyone who crosses paths with him. The Harrisburg area youth gravitate towards Bryan in an incredible way. The "Major Prep Mentality" Bryan preaches will continue to positively affect the lives of many. I will always speak highly of Bryan and continue to show my love and support in any way possible. Major Work, Major Results, Bryan is living proof!!
David Green, Jr.

I have known Bryan well over 20 years and can say he is truly one of the hardest working people I know. I have watched him take Major Prep from an idea to the level it is today through his grind alone. He is the definition of "practice what you preach" and puts in the work to get the results he seeks. I look forward to his growth and being a part of his Major Prep journey to success. Andre Watson, Friend and Brother

Bryan has grown into a great young man. He has the ability to affect any community in tremendous ways. He is easily able to connect with youth on a level that allows him to provide support and encouragement with their goals. Bryan's personal and professional characteristics shine in everything that he does, and we love him for that. Cece Pharris, Friend and Sister

I have known Bryan for over 20 years, and he has been a very influential person in my life. While so many people are blown away by the big dunks, crossovers, and other extravagant highlights of the game, Bryan has always been someone who appreciated the granular details like a player's footwork, spacing, timing, execution, etc. Bryan has always appreciated the fundamentals and applies this way of thinking to all aspects of his life, on and off the court. Bryan's leadership and diligent work ethic will serve as the catalyst that will positively impact today's youth and guide them on the path to reaching heights deemed impossible. Brian Smoot, Friend and Brother

ACKNOWLEDGMENTS

I greatly believe in the saying, 'It takes a village to raise a child,' mainly because I am a product of that. I first would like to thank my God for believing in me and helping me tap into the gifts and talents he put in me as He puts inside all of us.

I then would like to thank my loving parents, Merry-Grace Majors, who is the sole motivation for what I do in life and the late great Gary "Big Wes" Majors, who was the greatest man on earth in my eyes. I then have to thank my brothers, along with all of my family, friends, mentors, Goddaughters, nieces, and nephews, who have helped groom me into the man I am today. I want to thank Harrisburg, PA, for believing in Major Prep and giving me the confidence to move forward with the brand's goals and aspirations.

I have to send a special thank you to Dennise Hill & Madonna Awoti for challenging me as an author. Ana White, thank you for your sleepless nights, your time and effort into this project, you are FUEGO!!! Lastly, I must thank my college best friend, Marcus Burke, and my favorite college professor, MJ Fair, for always being supportive and playing an intricate role in my life and this project.

It's your boy, Bryan Majors, the owner of Major Preparation, where the motto is putting in Major Work for Major Results!

STAY FOCUSED, REMAIN HUMBLE & KEEP WORKING